How to Not Give a Shit and Not Be a Dumb Ass in the Process

The Ultimate Handbook on Being a Better Human

ISBN: 978-1-09836-346-8 (eBook)
ISBN: 978-1-09836-345-1 (Paperback)

First printing, 2021.

Printed by BookBaby, Inc., in the United States of America.

BookBaby
7905 N. Crescent Blvd.
Pennsauken, New Jersey, 08110

www.weaverofmyweb.com

For Mom.

Table of Contents

Preface

Many people are awakening and evolving spiritually. The symptoms mimic various things such as mental health issues—new, old, or exacerbated—and physical changes that look like various conditions such as the flu, which in itself can be scary, especially with the Coronavirus running rampant at the moment. There are lots of people coming into their "new" selves, so this and the relevant subject matters need to be discussed. There are many levels of spiritual growth and expansion, and this book will help those struggling in critical areas to prepare for these changes at the human level. Too many humans are having trouble with mental health—particularly, as it pertains to their spiritual health.

Psychology is the study of the mind, but the mind is a direct connection to the soul—the connection between our earthly existence and our connection to our higher selves, which, in effect, is our tether to a Higher Source. It is common knowledge that we are all made in God's likeness, as we are all God's children, but many people do not fully understand what this means. If we are extensions of God and God's presence in the Universe, why do we treat one another so horribly, and why do we have things like anxiety, depression, etc.? Are we saying

1

that God is depressed or has fears? Are we saying that God treats Her children badly, which makes it okay for us to do? Many questions can arise in people's minds when we allow these lower vibrating energies and thoughts to take over our lives. Instead, society has conditioned us to believe that God is only a sometimey afterthought or task—not a true way of being and worshipping.

Humankind needs help reconnecting with God and our Souls. There are cosmic, dimensional, and spiritual shifts happening, so merely going to church and reading the Bible is not enough at this juncture. These shifts are affecting our actions because our psyche is being affected and upgraded. We cannot remain in the mindsets and perspectives that we have been in for millennia, and we cannot force ourselves to stay in it any longer by using interventions that hinder our growth. When we try to enforce living in the world of Caesar, masking our true selves, or both, the Universe will force us to do its Will. It usually shows up in the forms we see—increased violence toward one another, wars, mental health imbalances, substance abuse to run from the despair felt in this reality, suicide, etc. We have to be who we were born to be despite what society wants of us or the traumatic experiences that were only meant to help us become stronger. Usually, the fight to be something we are not comes from the immense fear of disappointing others or their judgment. Fuck others and do you, as long as you are not hurting or killing other people; only God can tell you otherwise.

Although I will reference some of the ridiculousness going on in this current era of idiocy in our country as it relates to politics and racism, this is not a political book. However, I will talk about racism as it pertains to humanity and why it is

2

important that it has to end for everyone's sake, not just that of people of color. If this is a sensitive subject that will get your pressure up, do not read it—especially, if you are not mature enough in yourself to handle what is being said by positively doing something about it, irrespective of your color. I will also mention things of a religious nature and use Jesus as my point of reference since he is more widely known, but this is not a Sunday school lesson—well, not wholly anyway. I reference religion and Jesus a lot to poke holes in what some people like to hide behind to base their prejudices on by saying that this is what God wants for them to do. You do not have to believe in God to read this book. The messages will still apply to you. This is a real-people, real-world book, and I use personal experiences and what we are facing today in America as real-world examples of my messages on returning to a spiritually-centric humankind that doesn't give a shit about what you have, what you look like or how you live your private life. The book is not in any particular subject order but I hope it helps mold your thoughts and patterns throughout the reading. My biggest hope is that by the end of this book, you will be a more loving and open-thought person. If you are sensitive and cannot handle gutter language or truth of any kind, give this book to someone ready to hear these raw messages. Humanity is tired of individuals' selfishness and stupidity towards others, especially when it affects and is forced upon our private lives. The world is a beautiful soup made up of wonderful ingredients of different people of all subraces, shapes, sizes, and beliefs, and a menagerie of plant and wildlife supporting our existence. Every human is part of the same human race, and each life is equal in value. I will use the term "subrace" throughout this book to emphasize this when speaking of specific groups of people. If God did not want us to be free individual beings in this race, we would all have been created to be and look *completely* the same in every single way, down to the curls in our pubes. This world as we know it is not the same, nor are the people in it. It will never be the same again, nor will we, especially in this nation. We can no longer treat people horrendously because God made each of us special.

Over the ages, the patriarchy has been painting a selfish and strange world without compassion and empathy for others solely to ultimately cater to them, dressing it up as God's Will, through their free will. They have forgotten that this marble is made for and of various subraces and sexes of beings. This, alone, has purposefully ostracized many groups of people, marginalized many subraces, and set a precedent that it is and was okay to separate people on these bases, as long as you were a man doing it. It is time for that world to die away. Quite simply, this is an informal book of thought and spiritual exercise to attain a higher level of being for the betterment of humanity, but beginning with the individual. I will use simple prose and repurpose words to illustrate points so that anyone can absorb the information herein, and enjoy doing so. Also, I am a realist, so the events and language will be as such, alongside loads of facetiousness, sarcasm, and dry humor. There will be colloquialisms, some ungrammatical profundities, and very explicit language, but it is merely to vividly animate the malfeasance and nonfeasance in humankind and drive home the lessons.

I, also, will not supply tons of sources for a lot of my statements. However, naturally, I will cite any quotes and things of that nature, but my concepts or ideas and information that stem from common knowledge, I will not. I will *not* do someone's learning and research for them. We have developed into an intellectually lazy race of humans, and technology is to blame. I remember every question I had was answered by a book—whether one in an extensive collection of encyclopedias or a library. I spent years learning and reading about almost every subject matter that has crossed my path, and have exorbitant student loans like the next person. If any individual questions the veracity of any of this information, they can freely use whatever search engine or information-gathering medium they choose and do the research themselves; or, they can kindly contribute to my student loans and for publishing the additional pages, and I will research and teach whatever is thrown my way. I actually use my brain and only speak on things I firmly know and not just spew half-assed information for the masses to absorb. We have enough of that going on. I will always be sure that the information I convey will be sensible and valuable to the reader, so readers can be confident that the information they receive from this and subsequent media is balanced and truthful. We tend to judge the information out here based on whether or not there is empirical scientific data to support one's feelings and thoughts (which actually aren't scientific in origin). However, not everything has to be fact-checked against someone else's biased, and sometimes erroneous, information. It is up to us as individuals to learn on our own in order to understand the subject matter. At this point, can we trust *any* data that comes out? Science was originally about finding new ways to help humanity in understanding how things worked. Although many good scientists exist, science is now more about career progression, profit, and playing God or refuting Her existence, even to the detriment of innocent lives.

The same applies to some of the methods I recommend. I am not going to place sources for someone to learn how to meditate, for example, because there are many styles of doing so.

Prayer is a form of meditation but I am not going to give instructions or hunt down a YouTube video for you on how to pray and how to do it in an improved meditative way for your purpose. There are plenty of human sources, informational resources and media for everyone to tap to gain further knowledge of any given subject and to be their own investigative spiritual scientist to discover what spiritually works for them. I am not here to hold hands and teach anyone how to learn. I am simply here to provoke abstract thought of why we are here at this critical juncture and how to prepare yourself and your Soul to survive it. Since I mentioned it, prayer is a good place to start.

When I say "you," please use what you learned in school about context clues in a sentence to understand who I am referencing. Most times, it will be general or third person examples, while others will prompt you to think about yourself in that situation so you can see things from that point of view. You will see that I sometimes capitalize "Soul." This is not sloppy editing. It is purposely done when I am speaking about our Souls specifically, or not if I am just referencing souls in general. Lastly, but very importantly, I will refer to Allah/Creator/God/Source/Yahweh/etc. as "Her" or "She," as well as use these names interchangeably throughout this book. I will explain why in the *Duality & Reciprocity* section. However, if you know the Bible, you know it is explained in Genesis 5:1-2.

This book is my monologue—a colored rant voicing channeled messages for humanity to hear, and my life's grievances coming from my warped point of view. This book is a little therapy for me, also. It helped me to get thoughts and words out into the open that I would not have done otherwise. I know that I will be judged for my testicular fortitude in choosing to write this book and delivering these messages in this manner. Welp, I just don't give a shit, and these judgments prove the exact points that I make in this book. It is about the message, not the messenger, what they're wearing, who they are, who they sleep with, their past, or their subrace. Who cares that I use profanity. It's called freedom of speech. Externalities do not take away from the divinity of a message channeled from a higher place. If anyone who reads this is offended by anything I have written, I suggest looking at yourself to figure out why you are offended. However, the truth will *always* defend itself. There are plenty of books written by others who use vulgarity as marketing ploys but do they come from the struggles that a person like myself has come from? Do they understand the importance of being able to relate to their readers who have struggles, too, or is it simply to generate sales? I wrote this book because many people need to hear what no one else is saying in the manner that I am saying it, and they need to hear it from someone who has been through every single thing that I discuss (and, more!) in one way or another. Think of me as that awesome, unbiased neighbor who always has good words of advice or that candid friend you can always rely on to tell you the full truth, no matter how hurtful it may sound. Think of me as a drill sergeant and how harsh they can come off. They do it to push their cadets for discipline and strength to be prepared for what's out in the battlefield. I am doing this for the same reason—to push people to find their strength, no matter what they've endured in life, so that, as individuals, we can collectively work together to bring the good back to humanity in full force. Life is a battlefield, and if we are not well-equipped to fight the negative forces we face almost daily, we cannot and will not be collectively victorious.

We also do not need to hear how life can be made easy when it comes from people who have never or rarely experienced real-life hardships a day in their lives. I am a person who had hardships all their life, even suffering with some to date, yet I still made it through. As well-meaning as these people may be, we still need to, sometimes, be able to internally relate to those we wish to reach deeper in order to help them using our experiences—showing them that not only do we understand, but we have been there and got through it. "Let me show you how I did it so I can help you find a way to make it work for you!" Having difficulty in choosing which Balenciagas to wear on any given day is not a hardship. Figuring out everyday where your next meal is coming from when a lot of soup kitchens are closed or limited because of the 'rona, or hoping you won't be sleeping on a concrete bed the night the weather is calling for freezing temps or snow *is*.

I am not an angry or upset person by nature as the western world stereotypically believes of Black people—particularly, Black women. I am just tired of people, especially those who do not look like me, telling me that I need to be quiet or what I can do and say. I have surpassed my tolerance apex. I'm not letting anyone check me unless they're depositing. What I am is sympathetically mad as hell that these callous things are happening in humanity as innocent people are the ones who have to suffer for the actions of judgmentally uncaring and unthoughtful others. People who hurt people are what make me feel this way. People who take their problems and unresolved traumas out on innocent people is what bothers me. Individuals who do not have lane courtesy in life annoy me. People who think it is okay to disregard or take another person's life because they do not like the color of the other person's skin, because they

8

served your son a hotshot Belushi, because you don't want to live in fear by wearing a mask or staying the fuck home while you wait for your Covid test results, or simply because it is a Tuesday, disappoint me most of all. I love all souls, even those full of hatred and stupidity, but it is dumbfounding when people are deliberately hurt by others' actions. People may say that these things aren't deliberate. However, in fact, they are because there is always an option for the antagonist to do what is right from the start to avoid creating a bigger issue by being the bigger person. There is a duty in us all to implement the Golden Rule in our every action and have full accountability when we don't. Other people should not be our enemies. Together, we can do so much more to bring peace and prosperity to everyone, including ourselves. When we are constantly fighting one another or disrespecting the value of the life that God gave us, we will not be able to accomplish anything positive. We cannot continue living this way. It is not only for the sake of affecting other people's lives; it is for the sake of our own happiness as well. Our actions and others' lives are equally important and act in constant flux and reciprocity with each other. Our own lives are very precious, and the lives of others are equally so.

At the end of this book, I will include a list of books, videos or otherwise for people to read or watch that impacted my life and my view of my life as it pertains to the impact I am to make on this world through my experiences and words. They also led me to explore more of the world and to my purpose. I hope the same self-realization and vision for you all and that you all enjoy this book and really absorb the messages—not *how* they are conveyed or by whom. We have enough books and other mediums sugarcoating every word because everyone is so judgmental or sensitive. I am not here for your snowflake feelings or any schizo delusions. Your sensitivity is *your* concern. I am here, however, for people's growth and evolution because, somewhere and at some point, your decisions will affect my life, too—beyond buying this book—so I want to make sure the trajectory of those decisions comes from a positive energetic starting point so that I can return the positive energy to you in an unending cycle of love and light. Duality and Reciprocity at its finest!

Learning How to Not Give a Shit and Actually *Not* Giving a Shit

"*Most people are as happy as they make up their minds to be.*"
~ Abraham Lincoln

Not giving a shit about anything is the hardest thing a person can do, but once that skill is fully learned, a whole new world opens. We hear people say all day that they do not care about one thing or another, one way or the other, but most do not truly mean it at the soul level. One may say, "I don't give a shit," about something, then the very next second be worried about a bill that is past due when the bill collector rings; or, spending time reeling over their ex being with someone else; or, worrying about someone judging them for what they said or what they wore that day. I am not talking about being completely uncaring or unsympathetic to people's plights either. I am talking about being completely carefree. If we are not worried about bills, which we will die with, we are worried about other transitory things that have no bearing on our Soul's journey—like incessantly judging and worrying about other people and their lives or journeys, for example. When we do this, we take away

11

the positive, high vibrating energy we need to attain happiness and to live free of ego-based things, like disappointment. Although we are interconnected and interdependent, these things are usually trivial to our own paths and do not matter in the long run, or are completely irrelevant to our own growth. Bills, health concerns, and everyday life are not heavy enough whatsoever to lose faith or, ultimately, our Souls. Just as we have the capabilities to manifest our own destinies and dreams, we have the ability to control our perspectives on how we live our lives and attain our happiness. We create our own anxieties and stresses, or allow other people to give us their stress, by not having unwavering faith in Spirit and in our individual selves. Very simply, the narratives we create and live by are the same things that determine how our lives turn out.

If we live a life where we are constantly depressed or stressed and full of anxiety, we need to evaluate our perspectives on adverse events, and how we react to them when they arise. If you are one of these people and you hate feeling this way, ask yourself what you are actually doing about it. Most people will say, "Oh, I'm going to therapy and taking 'xyz' medication to help with my anxiety." My next question is *always*, "So, if you are taking these meds and have been taking them for years, why do you still have anxiety; or, if the meds and therapy don't work, why do you still take the meds and see this mental health team? Obviously, neither are working for you." The response is *always* a deer-in-headlights look or complete silence before they storm away in a temper tantrum or give me excuse #402 as they try to convince themselves that their anxiety is warranted and the meds are somehow helping, or it makes them believe they don't have anxiety when it is clearly still present when issues arise. It is said that 100% of a problem is 1% the problem itself and 99% how we react to the problem in reaching a solution. That perspective is a notch in the single key to living an eternally grateful life full of abundance and continual blessings. The problem is, most people do not know how to (or want to) be uncomfortable for a few minutes as opposed to a lifetime, forgive those that hurt us, let go of that hurt, or live with no expectations of outcomes— they do not know how to *not* give a shit. We unnecessarily add another or create a level of superficiality to our already complicated existence. You cannot say in one breath that you have full faith then allow yourself to stress or worry about anything in life or be sad about a disappointment in the next. You cannot live your life in full anxiety mode or stop living because of it. That is not a healthy way to exist, especially when it is totally unnecessary, while creating a scenario where you need anti-anxiety meds that are placebos or do absolutely nothing for one's mental state. Totally fucking backwards and it blows my mind in wonderment how people feel or think it is okay to live like this. It just makes zero sense to me and I refuse to try to understand it. There are no exceptions or special situations that require you to ever feel anxious or any other mental or physical disservice like this. What's the point of anxiety...what purpose does its existence in one's life serve? Most people I also ask this question say they don't know while popping their benzos to take them to zombieland. A positive life just does not come about or work this way, no matter how we try to justify our weaknesses. It is like saying you need to quit smoking while you are flicking your lighter and puffing your life away like a smokestack. You have to put in the actual work; it does not happen just because you say you are not going to do something. Everything has to be relinquished, the positive seen in unexpected events that have transpired and their outcomes, and, the Universe allowed to do its job to fix or reverse what happened—sans the anxiety, worrying about judgments or life's hardships, or having ill thoughts that depress the hell out of you—before you can reach any semblance of constant happiness. I will never understand why people love to be anxious, stress and worry then complain how they hate feeling those ways. I mean, they must love all of those heavy feelings if they aren't doing anything about them after all. Being dosed up on meds that stop people from feeling *anything* doesn't count. Being able to handle life without these drugs or bad habits are a part of the carefree goal we need to reach. If there is something in one's life that they do not like or that makes them feel unhappy, they have every freedom to change it or completely get rid of it. Doing nothing or the same old rigors of insanity is not conducive to growth or finding that happiness within. Why do we live in a society that has to be absent in order to live in the presence of reality? Life is not easy and no one promised it would be, but we must be stronger than our problems, or we miss out on happy moments in this state of being, also.

"Be believing, be happy, don't get discouraged. Things will work out."
~ Gordon B. Hinckley

Do you know what not giving a shit really feels like? I do not care if Susie and her trifling, judgmental clique does not like my outfit today. I could not care any less if the pious Mitchells next door know we are raising children in a same-sex household. I really wanted that house, but my offer was not accepted, so I am not shedding one damn tear and moving on to the next house because it was not the only structure built on this marble. I did not make my credit card payment this month because I was out of work because of the pandemic, and I am worried about my credit. Nope, I will not worry because it will get paid when they see the money, no matter when that is—especially since food and shelter are more important. Credit is a man-made institution of greed fixated on making the rich richer and those who need credit for survival forever indebted to these people; a system definitely not designed to be inclusive of certain persons. If banks and lenders are that uncaring when many people are struggling during these unprecedented times, then they are run by evil anyway and can go fuck themselves. The pearly gates do not have a minimum 800 credit score requirement for entry, so stop worrying that your 400 score won't allow you a seat on the bus. It feels good to not worry about anything and being able to sleep at night with no worries on our minds, particularly about things we cannot change in that moment. What happened to our faith in Source that we will not be left out on the street and starving (unless that is part of one's journey, which I will explain in a later chapter)? What happened to people valuing their Souls, and what happens to it, more than a creditor sending letters; or, what a neighbor says about their home lifestyle? Who gives a shit, really. I do not care about keeping up with the Joneses; I only care about keeping up with this Ryles. I have had to also learn not to care what family thinks because my journey is not theirs, and vice versa, happily cutting some off in the process to save my own happiness and sanity. Those same people we try to follow behind or be the people they want us to be have worries of their own and, on the inside, are unhappy about those worries, too. That is why we cannot take other people's journeys as our own or judge people if we do not know their journeys. The world is overflowing with enough people worried about all the wrong things when the Universe is strictly conspiring to give us our hearts' desires, all while pushing us to do God's Will, so we do not ever need to worry. We consistently choose to worry. Again, I'll ask, what is the purpose of worrying...what *positive* outcomes does it ever bring? The sole problem with our egos is a complete lack of faith in ourselves and, more importantly, in Source, so we create or rely on tangible things to have faith in just to have some semblance of control. We created this asinine idea in the Garden that we can and should make our own way, not believing in something we cannot see. We lost complete faith and found our egos. Humanity has been a mess ever since. If we let everything go, we would be so much happier, lighter and can help others reach this point, also. To fix this, every one of us needs to stop giving any fucks about dumb shit on this earth, stop trying to control other people's lives—especially, if playing God—and refocus on our own individual lives; all while living fully and being unconditionally happy throughout our individual journeys just as God intended for us to do for Her ultimate Will, not our own personal alternative life agenda.

So stop being sad because you did not get the house or job you wanted. The Universe has something better for you. The time you waste on being sad is time you waste not living by being disconnected from God and not experiencing true fulfillment and happiness. Stop worrying about your electric bill. Stop worrying about things that aren't there or have not happened yet. Stop worrying about any and everything. In short, stop worrying and stop giving a shit…the end! No more, no less. It's actually easy but we don't like to do easy things, clearly. People give themselves anxiety and stress themselves into an aneurysm over the same shit over and over, and never seem to get the lesson. These same people cry and whine about the fact that they have these stresses. Does worrying help you think through and solve the problem sensibly, or does it give you more anxiety, depression, hives, or ulcers? You instantly let your day be ruined because a bill collector called. Why...what can they do if your credit card or mortgage is overdue—come to your house and beat you to death in your sleep? Some people get petrified by bills...every single month, over and over and over again. It is a learned habit based on the crippling fear of insecurity or loss of socioeconomic status, which sometimes stems from judgments of other people anyway, but more on that in subsequent chapters. People stress over their health. As long as you are doing what you are supposed to do health-wise—eat healthy, exercise, maintain a healthy weight, and not stress at all—you will be okay. If a major illness develops then connect with God and make sure your Soul is ready. If God wants you, ain't shit your ass can do to stop Her, so why worry when you cannot do anything to change Her Will. If God needs you here, then the illness will go away as quickly as it came. We have seen some irony in this pandemic. It has taken some relatively healthy people longer to recover or out of this world completely. We can never know what God has planned but we cannot live a life full of anxiety because of the unknown. That is why faith in God is so important—more important than faith in our problems. We have faith in our employers who can impose layoffs at any moment paying us on Friday but don't believe God can remove the sources of our anxieties. Leave our troubles at Her feet and we will be okay is what is taught. We have to have faith and comfort in that.

Nevertheless, giving a shit about the wrong things is an unhealthy, earthly thing that will not matter later on. So, stop giving a shit, be carefree, and help others to do the same. It costs you nothing to do this but everything if you don't.

17

"I have no faith in human perfectibility. I think that human exertion will have no appreciable effect upon humanity. Man is now only more active-not more happy, nor more wise than he was 6,000 years ago."
~ Edgar Allen Poe

Duality and Reciprocity

Everything in the Universe, including Mother Nature, functions through duality. Duality is what we see in everything— the Yin and Yang, the masculine and feminine, the right and wrong, the night and day, the light and dark, the good and evil, the sun and moon...and the list goes on. You cannot have one without the other. Most notably is the masculine and feminine energy that we all embody and exists in everything. Source created us equal, possessing those equal energies. We all possess sacred masculine and divine feminine energy, but we must balance how much of each we harness. As a physical example, men produce estrogen and women produce testosterone, but at lower balanced levels than we produce our dominant reproductive hormone. Even Source is divinely proportioned as masculine and feminine energy; hence, how we are *all* made in Her/His likeness. The patriarchy has programmed us to believe that God was some old white man in the sky when She is actually the perfect balance of the masculine and feminine energy. God is neither one, but both. This is why I choose to address God as Her, as most address God as Him. Neither is wrong, but forcing people to believe that God is solely masculine is dangerous to one's Soul, an egregiously erroneous belief, and a blatantly wrongful interpretation of Logos. Nothing operates solely as one side, but together, they operate as one. This is pure balance. We cannot have anything one-sided as it takes both aspects of these energies for anything to work in harmony. Do we not have two arms, two legs, two eyes, two spheres of the brain, and so forth? This is the pathway to Nirvana...having a complete understanding of the Universe and the perfect balancing of these dual qualities while enveloping them in one's total being in order to reach complete happiness and peace. Once achieved, the one-track ego automatically falls away. God wants us to attain what She has gifted us at the beginning...eternal life in Her Kingdom. Allow the masculine and feminine to exist in whatever form it takes, as long as it is free-flowing in and from love. Humans are just formed dust particles that houses the light energy we return to when we transition, portraying this balance in genderless form.

Reciprocity is also a form of balance—an important one. We have to give, not take, in order to receive. When we give with a pure heart and with no intention to receive, we receive much more in return. My greatest personal example is from some years back when I was starving one particular late afternoon. I had only $20 left in my pocket because I had just started freelancing at the time. My partner and I went to a 'hood deli to get sandwiches. I said screw it and decided to treat us. The total came to about $12, leaving me with $8. I was overcharged about seventeen cents so I brought it to the clerk's attention. To some, it was just a few cents but, for me, it meant money that we did not have that we may have needed (I was in a different mindset back then but still remained who I am on the inside). We left after getting the money back. A few blocks away at a light on a four-lane boulevard, I watched a guy cross from the opposite intersection to my right, through the gas station on my immediate right, and directly to us as he bypassed lines of cars at all four points of this road. He asked if he could have some food. My partner initially said no to him, knowing that we were both broke—me, a freelancer and she not having any money until payday a few days away. He said, "Please?" The way he said it with extreme desperation and an upward inflection broke my heart into a million grains of hurt, so I told him to meet us back across the street at the 7-11—the original parking lot he came from before crossing the street to get to us. I told him to get whatever he wanted despite knowing I only had $8 and a couple of coins in my pocket. The store staff started harassing him, telling him he had to leave when he started pouring his fountain soda. They were very rude and indignant, so I said, "I am paying for his items, so back off; he just needs to eat." They looked at me inquisitively, wondering why I was doing that for him, an apparent junkie. The reason I did it was because he begged me for food...not money, not booze...but FOOD. Because he chose that lifestyle, is he not human enough to deserve food? Would Jesus have let him go hungry despite his lifestyle...so why would I? Everything he picked up, he asked if it was okay to buy. He picked up a pack of Oreos and asked if he could have it. I told him yes. He picked up a sandwich and asked. "I meant what I said; get what you want," I compassionately reassured him. He said he did not want to spend too much and he was just happy to eat because no one would feed him or let him in to get food. If I had to give him our sandwiches if the total went over, then I would have. The total, however, came to a few cents shy of $7. When we were done, he thanked me incessantly. I knew in my heart I did what was right, so no thanks was needed. However, I surely thanked God and him in my heart for giving me the opportunity to help him. I asked him what he would do for food later on and the day after and so forth. He replied that he would be okay, and we parted ways, thanking each other in silence, as I watched him disappear down the opposite business street.

"*Happiness is not something ready-made. It comes from your own actions.*"
~ Dalai Lama

My partner had witnessed the whole encounter unbeknownst to me and was crying her eyeballs out because she had never seen anyone do that before—particularly, how he approached us out of all of the choices of cars he could have stopped at during rush hour at a busy intersection or the people pumping gas next to us. A few days later, I received a few deals that put a couple of stacks in my pocket. It was an entirely heart-wrenching situation that I still tear up about because he was just so innocently hungry, and no one would feed him. In case you're asking right now, yes, we live in a country that denies people food or will throw it away before they feed someone who is hungry just because they cannot pay for it. However, the equally worst part is that I always get funny looks for doing what I did as if it is weird or wrong to feed people in the street or give them company where they are and words of encouragement, in addition to a couple coins if one has it to spare. Sometimes all you have to do is show up and say yes to the opportunities to bless someone else that God presents to you, most times as a test—even if in the moment we are not aware that we are being tested. Would I block God from receiving food if I could help...so why would I turn him away? These situations can no longer be seen as tests for me if my answer is always the same. They become opportunities to prove to our Creator and myself that the well-being of humanity is still important to me, despite the constant disappointments from only a handful of individuals, relatively speaking. My heart was so full after that, and I did not give a corner of a fuck that other people were weirdly judging me for it. The feeling was so immense that I am crying writing this. This type of fulfillment and happiness from altruism cannot be bought, especially when it helps someone else first. This is the exact feeling we can feel every time we employ the Golden Rule—even in the smallest way. Fulfillment is what we long for when we develop bad habits to fill voids. Also, please keep in mind that there are some shysters who want a quick dollar, knowing they have a home and are just too high or drunk to work. I recommend using your discernment (not personal judgment) to determine who is just trying to buy drugs or booze and who is truly down on their luck.

Always freely give without expectations of receiving because God is an infinite Source (hence, the name) and will always reward you for doing good for others. You never know what angels She sends here to test you in a moment, like She tested Lot in his moment. I have had many of these moments. I always responded with altruism and was supernaturally blessed for it. Keep in mind, this is not why I do it. I do it because of the feeling that giving and helping people gives me. The feeling that comes from reciprocity. That is the instant reward I receive first after giving joy to another person. Seeing the look on a person's face that knows they are not going to starve that night is priceless, especially when they are children or seniors. I have been that person before, and it is sickening how people of this world will let another human starve because of their own biases, selfishness or pure unadulterated greed.

"I don't want to get to the end of my life and find that I have lived just the length of it. I want to have lived the width of it as well."

~ Diane Ackerman

What is Nirvana, and how does one get there?

A Soul's destination on earth is to reach total attainment, or Nirvana. Follow Logos, and there will be no question of reaching the spiritual level Buddha, Jesus, and Muhammad (and some unknown others) reached. Nirvana is the release from the cycle of life and death, and reaching a state of perfect happiness and peace. This must happen before one's earthly Circle of Life completes its cycle. If one does not complete their work while here on this plane, they are destined to come back to repeat the lessons until they are learned, suffering through life's trials once again. The concept of Nirvana is a Buddhist teaching, but this final goal is the exact interpretation of the purpose of humanity's evolution and the entire journey that is the basis of almost all teachings.

There is only one way to reach Nirvana—through being Christ-like. I am not saying this from a Christian point of view; I am saying this from a righteousness point of view. We have already defined who and what Jesus was and who he is to us today. Jesus and the others have similar stories that provide us with the blueprint to building a wonderful life that all people can learn from. We cannot say we are Christ-like then lie, steal, or kill for such trivial reasons. We cannot say we are Christ-like and treat others horribly. We have to embody one hundred percent of the Christ that is laid out for us. We have to do every single thing in every part of our life in the quest to reach Nirvana. This is why so many do not reach this level. We cannot have one iota of hatred in our hearts, no matter how pressed we are to justify our biases. We cannot treat anyone any differently for any reason, even if they have wronged us. *This* is the absolute hardest one for people to do and what damns them every time because it requires forgiveness and letting go. We cannot say we are Christ-like then, in the same breath, say we hate someone or we want to do/actually do or wish harm on someone for hurting us. That is Karma's job, and She will do a hell of a lot more damage than any human can ever inflict. We have to live kindly in nature to every single living soul and thing, not just to the people we bang with.

When we hold on to any energetic vibration that is lower than where we vibrate, we will never be able to elevate higher than that vibration, not without more work than would be needed if we were not holding on to those things. Nirvana is returning to the pure light that we were before entering this plane. This is the same illuminating light that is always seen around Jesus in (erroneous) historical depictions of him. Reaching Nirvana is the very definition of *ascending to Heaven*. Light ascends because it is light, not heavy. It does not have any particle of heavy energy in it, or else it would not be light in both the physical and ethereal senses. This is a very esoteric subject, and most will not be open to or grasp this concept, but those who are awakened even just a little will understand this interpretation. However, even some of those who are newly awakened are still at a critical point where it is easy to fall back to earth from the slightest of hardships or judgments. These things are low-vibrating, and the more awake we are to the Universe, the more we are exposed to so that the other half of the dual power has its run on dimming our lights. We must stay vigilant; we must stay strong. We have to protect our Light at all costs and help others reach their brightest. It is an important matter culminating in where our Souls end up at our Sunsets.

Judgment—Racism, Social Issues, and Our Human Duties

This section will be a heavy one to digest because it is a sensitive area for many, but let's just dive in. Becoming a judge and executioner by one's own appointment is never okay. Far too many people are taking these roles when they are not asked or required to, or out of spite in retaliation of events from their past. The bad apples in our society who have been appointed these positions by profession (lawyers, judges, L.E.O.s, etc.) come from the same pool of fearful, hateful individuals who have absolutely no business being in public service. Unfortunately, these are also the people who have a concerted biased control over certain people's lives, carrying on exhausting efforts of the social nemesis we are combatting today. Often, they make an oath based on religion when church and state should always be separate, adding another layer of bias to an already one-sided system. You cannot impose laws and regulations that have an underlying tether to the problems that continue to subsist and plague our land to date. You also cannot base laws on a religion that has been misinterpreted over many millennia and that not all people follow. These are antiquated traps enforced to keep the aforementioned marginalized groups from progress. There is hardly any real effort, other than when required per case, to ameliorate or rewrite old legislature and precedents that were established specifically for the sole purpose of giving a blatant advantage to one side and not another. Judgments, especially in law, aren't always fair or true just because of the source (look at any case involvng a Black person wrongfully accused or forced to choose the lesser evil and plead guilty just to be treated as a human being, like 15 year-old Saraya Rees). This is just another downplayed cog in the socially unjust impetus for racism's program. This is also why Black people need to be more cognizant of the importance of an education since we are more likely to end up in these situations, and presented with legalese that is likely to confuse or frustrate us into choosing the wrong path—as is intended. In working with ex-offenders periodically, I found that, sometimes, we do the work for the oppressor then we are angered at the fact that we didn't know enough to prevent, or lessen, the oppression. There is a glimmer of hope, however, with judges like Judge Carlos Moore in Florida who makes use of a different, yet a most effective, approach to criminal rehabilitation by not making a negative "example" out of his cases like some judges do—particularly, in cases involving Black offenders. Get to know this trailblazer in law.

We cannot continue to habitually or inadvertently judge others. Judgment of one's decisions is not for us to do. What one does behind closed doors is not your business to judge as right or wrong. What one does with their own body is not your business either, especially the men who believe they can tell a woman what to do with hers and passing enforceable laws justifying their personal reasons why women should be put in this place. If I ever *need* or want these chauvinistic lawmakers and their supporting female idiot cast of colleagues in my nether regions, front or back, I will send them a personal invite to gather there or to kiss there—dealer's choice which. Again, just because one claims "Christian," it does not mean their actions and beliefs are aligned with good or righteousness, nor should be deemed good for the whole of groups of people. Religion is what muddies laws that are made for everyone and makes the world hyper-biased. If a woman gets pregnant and cannot afford any more children, does not want any more children, or whatever her reasoning is, she should have the right to abort. The end. There should never be laws in place that prohibit a woman from doing whatever they want with her own person. It is her God-given right to procreate or not and her business to deal with God for any consequences. Just because a lawmaker has this archaic view, it does not give them the right to impose it on others. This example goes deeper than religious beliefs and is another token for women being out of "man" business and staying in their rightful places—"barefoot and pregnant." I use this example because it is the most idiotic thing men and stupid women have fallen in line with and supported as a form of control, based on the belief that a clump of cells have rights. As an African-American woman, I take extreme exception to this because it makes me think that a clump of cells, that could easily be deemed a cyst before its first heartbeat, has more life value than I do as an educated Black female human being that is already here in existence in a country that has hated the likes of me since before I existed. What a disgusting insult, but it is to be expected from the type of people writing these laws; they're usually all the same, touting religious beliefs to justify their heinous controlling acts on their own constituents.

Judgment is not all about law or justice, however. We judge people constantly throughout our day, and, because it has become so naturalized in our day-to-day, we do it autonomously.

30

From judging someone's picture on social media to judging what someone wore to work today to a friend's decision to have a sex change. None of these decisions are ours to make, nor are they ours to judge. If we did not judge a person by their external features, we would only be left to judge them by their character, as Dr. Martin Luther King, Jr. and the Bible said, and as it is supposed to be. I cannot stress enough how important it is to *not* judge people as it affects our own happiness and, ultimately, our Soul's Journey, as well as those around us. Yes, *you* judging someone else affects your own happiness! If you're judging someone, it is usually not in a positive context. In fact, judging is mostly done when a "wrong" has been committed. Generally, how often do you hear a positive judgment about someone wearing white after Labor Day? I have witnessed this in my own personal experiences over the years, but not many people can say that they often hear positive respects to someone when this alleged fashion faux pas occurs. The consensus about this old ass thought is usually the same, especially in older generations. Conversely, as with everything else we have turned around over time to make it socially acceptable when convenient, this idea was of practical function in its origin and of the same premise as not wearing black in summer. White, or bright clothing, deflects sunlight, thus it is better to be worn in warmer weather to keep the person cooler overall; and, vice versa for black in summer and only wearing it in cooler months. Labor Day is deemed the unofficial end of summer; thus, also, warmer weather. Over time, it evolved into a fashion taboo. We actually shamed people for wearing white after Labor Day for the longest time. Only in recent years have we seen changes in the attitude towards this. However, let us consider how many people, for example, who may have already been struggling with self-esteem issues, had to suffer from people's judgments over something that was entirely different to begin with. It was originally a suggestion and completely up to the wearer, not a mandatory fashion regulation.

Although happiness is subjective, it is also objective. We have to stop judging people based on our own skewed views of what right and wrong or good and bad/evil is. These are also subjective and projected on to others like our judgments. It is taboo to wear flip flops to work. Does that choice of comfortable shoe stop the person from successfully doing their job as a Certified Public Accountant? No, but that person's abilities and character are devalued because of what they decided to wear to be comfortable that day, possibly due to a bunion or just for the hell of it. How does any of that make sense in any way? Whatever their reason for it is *their* reason for it, not yours or your decision, and it does not mean that their breathing toes are going to stop them from calculating a company's Ebitda.

There are many varying levels of growth from constant judgment. Experiencing and learning new things, exploring new opportunities, and shedding bad habits, old paradigms, and toxic people are all ways we can move forward to ultimately gain happiness and peace. We have all gone through this at some point in life but not usually with intent and purpose. In fact, most people have an unhealthy fear and view of change, usually coupled with the same type of view of themselves. It is agreed that change is scary, but many will fight the reasoning that it is necessary if one is in belief that they are fine and happy the way that they are, no matter how dangerous or mentally unbalanced they happen to be. Change isn't just for the person going through it; it is for everyone. It only takes one person to start the wave.

"Thousands of candles can be lighted from a single candle, and the life of the candle will not be shortened. Happiness never decreases by being shared."
~Buddha

On another front, we look at the state of this country in terms of how people have significantly changed since our 2016 presidential election and politics in general. All politics is a circus. You have a ring leader in the most important position, making calls for the whole constituency. It is all a massive, profitable joke to these people, and human lives are seriously at stake. We were taught to play this sick game at a very young age, without even knowing the actual definition of politics. Still, we were forced to play nice and share with everyone no matter how we felt about them on the same playgrounds behind these "educational" institutions. We were primed to hate one another's different views first and respect each other second, unless we had the same views or same physical characteristics. No wonder people are confused about life because brainwashing started so early in development despite what they felt inside to be right. Children are not born with hateful ideals—they are taught. People have turned into finger-pointing schoolyard idiots just to be able to say their political party is better than the other. I have never seen so much immaturity in my life. The conversations sound like:

Right boy: My teacher is better than your teacher because we get to have recess all day and laugh at you because you don't; he also doesn't punish us like your stupid teacher does when we bully the retarded girl with the braces.

Left girl: Well, our teacher keeps us in more often and gives us homework so we can learn more. We are taught tolerance and to respect other people, regardless of our differences. Also, your teacher is an idiot.

Right boy: No, he's not. Learning is a violation of my right to play and have fun, and I do not have to learn if I don't want to. I hate school. He understands that we are oppressed by the school system. He also doesn't let my victim, Omar, tell my parents I stuffed him in the locker. I can get away with everything, and my teacher doesn't care. He is so cool, and you are a radical left for not liking him; therefore, our enemy.

Left girl: The point of school is to learn so that you can do better for yourself, learn about and live alongside other people, and overall positively contribute to society. Why are you so concerned about bullying Omar? He has not done anything to you.

Right boy: Well...What about Mr. Johnson from Kindergarten? He made things bad for our teacher even though this is his first year in our school, and Mr. Johnson retired five years ago. It's all his fault, though. Our teacher, Mr. Dumass, said so, and he would not lie to us. Omar doesn't look like me, so my teacher told me I should treat him this way. We don't like "different" people.

Left girl: Our way isn't for everyone and we are still fallible humans but your way just sounds selfish and stupid, and quite a bit intolerant.

Right boy: This is why girls shouldn't be allowed to run for student council. They will give away our rights to bully people who are different and don't listen to us men or do what we tell them. Girls and the left will give away our right to play in the dirt all day to immigrants, and there won't be any more sand in the desert for us to have. We brought this sand here from other playgrounds we stole it from. It is ours to do what we want because Jesus said we could.

What a bumbling mess. This is the actual context of the exchanges between the "right" and the "left." At least, this is what I hear and see when they speak to or talk about each other. What the hell is a right and a left anyway, why is this a thing, and why are there hundreds of subcategories of this crap? When the Notorious RBG passed away, people could not wait to jump all over the opportunity to bring up politics. A great female fighter for equality—especially in jurisprudence, a pioneer and teacher lost their battle with cancer, and, four minutes after it was announced, all people could be concerned with was who would replace her while food fighting across the aisles like middle schoolers. This is the immature, unfeeling world we live in. I thought politics was about doing what is in the best interest of *all* parts of society. Why are millionaires and billionaires fighting us over paying taxes? In general, the amount of taxes they need to pay is barely a whole percent of their wealth, and they are complaining as if it will put them in the poorhouse like 97-99% of the rest of the people in this country that actually are. Why are people fighting about some of their taxes going to food stamps? Every human being needs food. If one can fervently argue that food stamps are a drain on society and should be cut out while they don't peep when billion dollar corporations with substantial cash reserves are bailed out, then I am embarrassed as a human for them. Arguing that these people need to get jobs is not a resolution because a good portion of the recipients are the disabled, seniors, and people who cannot afford food because they are paying more in taxes than the rich. Let alone the fact they are people who are victims of a system that put them in this position to begin with, but starving them even more is the solution you have for this. Great! We will let all the grandmothers who spent their time working and raising families a great deal of their 70-plus years here know how you feel about their lazy asses on food stamps. I am sure a lot of the complainers' grandmothers are included in this number, by the way. Or, maybe not if they are a millionaire or billionaire hoarding money. Also, if some believe that gun rights are paramount because they have this schizo-based fear that all Black people are going to bust down their sole door for all of the racist shit their ancestors ever did, and they need to protect themselves and their family, then they have a lot of educating themselves on humanity and internal work to do. We are too busy fighting to protect our own damn lives, and our children's lives, from people like them to devise plans with every other person of color to care about looking for them in their trailer parks. Delusions of being more important than any other group of people should not *ever* trump starvation. There is actually a word for this, but I am tired of using it and seeing it, keeping myself in that energy in the discussion of others, so it has no place in this book. The bottom line is that the people making decisions for the collective are the ones using their own personal agendas to form our realities. Fix this insanity, people!

"I will permit no man to narrow or degrade my soul by making me hate him."

~ Booker T. Washington

Make no mistake, my people are not exempt from this dumb shit. Our judgment just comes in a different form. This isn't all Black people, just like it isn't all White people who are racist. Some Black people have a tendency to use systemic oppression as a crutch to be lazy asses. They also choose not to be better people when they are out here uneducated or rude as hell for no reason at all on the one end, or standing on the corner selling drugs or murdering us for material or no reason at all on the other. I understand we are angry, but being murderous of our own people, rude to our own people, stealing from our own people, or remaining uneducated are no reasons at all to treat any person these ways at any given time, regardless of color. Killing each other because they know no better as their individual reason to be in the street keeps us in the same position as a people. Black people will see other Black people and hate on them in disgust because they have excelled. An example of this is a Black college boy getting good grades, presented a nice car for those good grades, and getting a very good job after graduating, and he is murdered because his childhood friend that dropped out to sell drugs on the street was jealous because he chose to remain in the streets, instead of doing better. Another example is a female killing another female without asking questions because she sees the other chick with her boyfriend. A final example is a drive-by shooting at a car that looks like the one their enemy drives when the victim was someone completely innocent that just happened to drive the same type of car as if the idiotic murderer didn't know that there were more cars and drivers on the road than just that one they hated. There is nothing in the world so important that anyone has to take another person's life, not even if they feel it is justified. Shortening another's life is not anyone's judgment to make. There is never any justification for murder. Period! Self-defense is another thing; it is not murder.

If this is your mindset, I am speaking to you now. I do not care if a person disrespects you. Grow up, maintain your own respect, and simply stop associating with people that attempt to take it away. I do not care if they stole your significant other. The person was probably not worth it in the first place. I do not care if you wanted the shoes they had on. Complete your education, get a job with a W-2, a gig that doesn't require you to secretly meet your boss in an alley, or start a business that is not classified as door-to-door ganja salesman, and go buy the shit yourself. Higher education is not for everyone, I agree. I didn't care for the grueling work or the establishment behind this country's entire educational system, despite my academic accomplishments, but please don't be 30 years old without at least a high school diploma or G.E.D. Some things are inexcusable. After that, you can be the boss someone meets in the alley...of your auto shop business, or sell all the ganja you want out of your legal cannabis brick and mortar.

I do not care if you just felt like doing harm to that person. If you think it's cute, funny, or cool standing on the corner, selling drugs or murdering people because your friends or gang peers said so...it is not. Your 60-year-old self is looking back at you in pure disdain and utter disappointment. You deserve nothing except a life in prison for every year your victim lived to rehabilitate and reconsider your actions. We are already deemed barbaric and uneducated, so thank you for continuing to be part of the problem that makes us look bad. If you do not want your life, go be stupid elsewhere. Some of us are trying to live and be treated like humans, and not be wrestling dummies for cops and target practice for thugs too lazy or small-minded to get an education, careers, or jobs—anything positive and productive. I used the word "thugs" irrespective of color because that is exactly what you are if you can murder someone in cold blood for useless pettiness—Q'uan on the corner or the white cop killing another black man, alike. Those who do not commit murder but, instead, kidnap, molest/rape, sell drugs that kill people, or any other harmful acts are included in this lot because you are doing physical harm to others—even if they solicit you for it. You are there to provide that harm that does not help you or your victim.

There are many corners that birthed hip-hop and some labels, clothing lines, dance legends, acting and singing careers, and inspired individuals to do more positive in society. Everyone was living and *being* free during those times. Now, it is something else. Typically, if your life is spent on a street corner, there is doubt you are selling your talent...to the right people, anyway. People have become desensitized and complacent with the amount of crime in our communities. They see these moving lampposts as regular pharmacy fixtures with the keys to lala land. It is almost like it's expected and normalized. Murder, other forms of violence, and substance abuse should never be normal occurrences. There are, also, many hard-working Black people employed in thankless hourly positions at places that people love to patronize, yet get very little recognition for. This list includes the barista or clerk at your favorite coffee shop, grocer, or other frequented store, dealing with people's attitudes when their coffee isn't scalding hot enough, or because the price of cheese went up at the grocery store; the janitors and security guards tirelessly sanitizing or securing your hospitals or office buildings full of rich executives and lawyers, especially during Covid; the nurses, medical technicians, et al. who work doubles and triples changing shitty diapers on invalids or generally do all of the dirty work for the doctors, exposing themselves to all types of anything, but get paid a hell of a lot less; or, the waitress making $2 an hour at your favorite restaurant trying to pay her way through college, but she doesn't get a tip because the cook gave you cold, greasy fries or soggy lettuce on your burger. I can go on. These are the positions we seem to hold most often because we constantly meet ceilings that are consistently being raised or doors with locks that keep changing. The change in this direction over the recent years has been long overdue as more companies implement diversity, equity and inclusion in their governance, but we still have a long way to go with tons of work yet to be done.

The point is, people of color have always kept this country going and have been killed by thugs or, otherwise, treated like shit by others. We do not need more bad people committing nefarious acts to add to our plight, and prefer they find kindred Souls, go to an island, and do that shit to each other. I see why White people often tell us to go back to Africa when we act like wild animals running through the streets killing each other; albeit, for a different reason. I would tell them the same shit, too, if they were just wantonly killing people. Simultaneously, these barbaric cops who kill us like we are prey in the wild can club their meal until their heart's content. Neither one is any different than the other. They should join forces. I love them as humans and know they can be rehabilitated because they are likely a product of their environment just like racists are, but I do not have to like living with them. If they do not want to be rehabilitated, I hear Guantanamo Bay is nice this time of year...they should feel free to go to be treated like they treat others, and make it a first-class JPATS trip when they go. We do not need them here on the streets with our children nor our seniors. We have enough struggles and extra worries in life. *This* subject really angers me because we cannot freely walk out of our doors without wondering if we will get shot by a thug's bullet or if we will get pulled over and get shot by a law enforcement thug's bullet. We need to do better as a people in the same struggle to get to the same peaceful end by refocusing our anger into positive processes, not work against each other to get to no end of this treatment. There have been Black people who have said this before to other Black people. These courageous and honest Black people have been called traitors to our struggle because we do not support *why* these thugs do what they do. Why should Black people support murderers of our own kind, just because we share an impetus? Is this something we are supposed to accept just because we are in the same struggle? These thugs could not care any less about an innocent life, but they expect to be treated by other Black people with respect and sympathy because of the struggle. GTFOH! Respect is earned, and our murdered relatives can no longer speak to this respect.

The hurtful reality is Black people have been used and abused for so long, without equal gratitude and respect, that we have forgotten our true identities. Special parts of our culture have been exploited or stolen, and sometimes denigrated, for profit. Caucasians built this current world on the backs of people of color or through gangster-like thievery that is legal only if perpetrated by them. Black and Indigenous Peoples of Color (BIPOCs) have had our lands stolen, our livelihoods desecrated (picture it: Greenwood District, 1921- another fuckin massacre on Black people), and have been murdered during these robberies, especially if we fought back in any way. This is similar to how they used their guns to fervently protect what they stole. I guess this is where the paranoia comes in. How can apartheid have been a thing on our own lands? How can an invading subrace tell us we do not belong in our own countries? Then, when we flee, we are not welcomed anywhere and told to go back to our "shithole countries" that became that way when these same people ravaged our beautiful lands and abundant resources for profit without equally giving back to the parties they were stolen from. This seems like a one-sided bash but I am merely reiterating what we already know from history.

All over the world, people of color have suffered at the hands of or as a result of the actions of one subrace. Some have self-proclaimed themselves as a "master race," but they are not. They are part of the same damn race of humans as everyone else—nor better than anyone else in any respects. Every human, despite color, has special gifts or talents. This small band of people's narcissistic delusions of grandeur are laughable, and it is hard not to believe that a great many of the people in this herd with this belief, no matter how slight, are schizophrenic in some way. In a way, it is self-fulfilling as it reflects their immense fear that the centuries of ravaging lands and people will come back to bite them in the ass. You cannot go bullying your way around the world starting wars, killing indigenous peoples and claiming lands that do not belong to you in the name of freedom and power, and not expect any repercussions because you claim you are better than the lives you've stolen with "Christian" justification. When people outside of this subrace, and those who are part of this subrace but do not share this outrageous belief of superiority, challenge this group in any way, deflection is their first line of defense, and we are deemed dangerous racial terrorists or treasonous to that subrace. Last I checked, we are the only ones being killed off by some people in this group just because of our skin color or those of this subrace rocking out with us in our struggle sadly experiencing our deadly outcomes by people of their own race. They have not been legally murdering any other subraces at large in this country. We do not see police storming into an Irish household, shooting it up then being acquitted for their unnecessary casualties. We do not see Far East Asian Americans being consistently profiled and pulled over by the cars they drive or chastised for how they wear their clothes, then locked up for living. We are tired of systematically being picked off in a country we, quite literally, *slaved* to build, and it being normalized by this same subrace with the world being told that racism only exists in people of color or that it does not exist at all. These are the same people who also avow being Christ-like and are the most devout of Christians.

We are constantly criticized when we point out their racism with them calling it race-baiting or "pulling the race card." We do not have time to share in your ridiculousness, White people. If we are pulling the damn card, you likely shuffled the deck and dealt the hand—the aforementioned deflection in plain view. Some of these Caucasians are quick to be callous and evil as shit when their "supremacy" is challenged or their pilfered "privilege" threatened when they are confronted with their demons. The person or persons who point these things out are, instead, demonized. Additionally, one of the most irritating things "Karen and Chad" supporters do on social media when the perpetrator pays for their racist acts (losing high profile jobs or other positions, their personal info spread online, etc.) is joining in the shaming by saying that their punishment was too harsh. I agree we cannot continue to fight hate with more hate by going

43

to their homes and causing them or their families any harm. However, I wholeheartedly disagree that racist people in high profile positions who likely make decisions that affect the lives of people of color should not lose their jobs. That is the start of weeding out perpetuated systemic racism in organizations that control, or predominantly control, the way our country is run. The irony is, when a person of color is the perpetrator, within minutes, no matter how successful they were, he/she will have their name dragged through the mud and a slew of people saying he/she should be hung or a noose symbolically placed in their environment. "Boy, know your place," being spray-painted somewhere nearby the noose.

We can no longer use the excuses from decades or centuries ago that black people are criminals, lazy, dirty, or inferior. You really have to look into your heart and ask why so much hate for another subrace, or humans rather, exists. Why do you dislike a whole subrace that personally did nothing to you? If you think you have a valid answer, double-check where it comes from—more racism, stereotypes, shared peer feelings, etc. If you have absolutely no valid reason why, yet you choose not to help fight to right the wrongs, then you need to look within and figure out where and why that type of hate exists to keep you inactive—shared peer feelings again, major insecurities, pure unabashed ignorance, etc. If you think it is okay or Christian-like to have this hatred, you're delusional. It is never okay. Our inner Jesus cannot exist in the same space as hatred, and believing it can is blasphemous. God's Love cannot exist with hate. While you run and gun down Black people in your neighborhood just for existing in it, ask yourself if Jesus would be sitting next to you, smiling, while shining his .45 carbine, telling you he couldn't wait to pick another one off. Is he really smiling at you in pride for this or utter disappointment? How would you feel if you found out these actions heavily disappointed Jesus? Can you still call yourself Christian in his eyes...or will you just shoot him, too, because you realized Jesus was colored and sitting next to you? I mean, how dare the man Christians worship be colored, right? It's an outright abomination for a colored man to be the one to preach that we are all equal in God's eyes. The audacity and blatant irony. Who does Karen complain to to have the Bible and history books changed to reflect the White Jesus she knows?

The method of silencing us and removing our humanity is stifling and taking away our lives, strengths, and our voices by any means. In this fairly new century and millennium, it now comes in the form of police brutality as opposed to lynching, maiming, or castration, so we cannot bring more strong, resilient brothers and sisters into this world. These actions are based on fear of losing what was stolen by them in the first place. A thief will kill to get what they want, then kill again to protect what they already killed for. These are not good types of people. Not everything can belong to one person or the same group of people. No human on this planet is superior to another or entitled to owning the planet that greed is destroying. No one! We all have special individual characteristics, gifts, and talents by design. We do not need to kill the next person, or persons, because we are too lazy to cultivate and engage our own God-given gifts or because we are flat out jealous of the next individual that is seen as special in some way. We absolutely cannot under any circumstances lower our vibrations and standards as human beings when we act this way. It just adds to the heaviness of our plight as humans, and all of those before us who senselessly lost their lives because of these ignorant souls would have died for absolutely nothing. The more I see that we are all no different, the more humanity proves that we are all the same.

It feels like in the past 50-plus years since Dr. Martin Luther King, Jr. was assassinated, Black people have not made any real racial progress because we are still fighting every day with the police and bigoted vigilantes for our lives. Being able to use the same toilet as others is not what we call progress. We have been hunted and killed like animals for far too long. We are not game; we are human fucking beings. We are demanding our humanity back, but we must do it the right way, not full of anger and resentment for an entire subrace of people. We must use our anger as passion and put the blame where it belongs, in the right ways. The biggest struggle, it seems, is getting the government on our side to help in this fight, considering *some* of the greedy, lazy forefathers who founded this country created the premise that Blacks are to indefinitely be property and used as slaves for our backs and aided in the erosion of our subrace on this soil. We certainly must not forget that the Indians and Mexicans who were here before any of us came with our racial drama were treated as horrendously as we were when this was their land first. It was clearly stolen from them, but history only paints them as savages and deserving to be caged and killed for this beautiful land that is large enough to share. There are many depictions of the Indians and settlers working together, but for whose one-sided benefit though? We are all in this fight, and we will not stop until we receive reparations in the form of equality (money or equal soil always helps) for all the callous events over the past several centuries. That is all we wanted from the start—just to be equal and treated as such. The only difference is we will not be the hateful savages they painted us as this time. We are better than these bad actors in the way we treat one another and how history

46

has painted people of color, especially those who were savagely killed in the name of greed. This message is primarily for my brothers and sisters who think it is cool, cute, or fun to kill one another for stupid reasons but, more so, to the opposition who still think that Black people were only created to tend their family plantations, as human targets for practice, mules, or as sexual objects.

"The first time any man's freedom is trodden on, we're all damaged."
~ Captain Jean Luc Picard

Recently, there has been backlash geared toward Netflix about the movie "Cuties." The French movie is said to hypersexualize teenage girls, and the sentiment is that Netflix is complicit in child sex trafficking and aiding pedophilia while peddling child pornography. This is a very long stretch. Whenever problems are brought to the forefront, people go ham, saying, "Oh my God, you cannot show this because it is socially unacceptable." Child sex trafficking is unacceptable in *every* way, but how and why is a movie socially unacceptable that shows society what really goes on so that people are aware? So, knowledge is unacceptable now? How do we fix a problem unbeknownst to us if we do not know of its existence? When are we supposed to talk about it? Sweeping things under a rug because people are too sensitive to address the issues head-on exacerbates the problem, and *you* become complicit—not those making us aware.

There are actually ignorant souls who do not know, or want to know, these problems exist or are constantly ignoring the crux of the problem but committed to expending all energy to fight the mediums used to reveal it to them. Bringing existing problems to the world's attention in the form of art is the same premise I had for this book. We cannot continue to ignore problems because the world is sensitive to issues that the world is not collectively standing together to continually fight. We complain but think canceling a streaming subscription that eventually will be reinstated is the best form of protest. No. It is asinine like 99% of the rest of the habits and ways of thinking the world employs. *Oh my God, I am canceling my Disney subscription because they showed some of the original suspect anti-Semitic cartoons, yet I am actively not doing anything to fight anti-Semitism. Oh my God, don't show my children, "Eyes on the Prize," because it shows racism in its truest form, or else I am blocking PBS on my television, or taking my already oblivious children out of school so they don't see racism's true face.* If we do not fully understand a problem or know of its prevalent existence, how can it be fixed? If your idea of fixing a problem is canceling a streaming service, then you have no other meaningful suggestions to add to the conversation, or to society. These individuals are the same types of people who think "All Lives Matter" is more important than understanding Black Lives Matter (BLM)'s principle argument. They are complete simpletons, and add to the problems we have with bringing racism to the forefront and making people address their bigotry.

When people disregard the reason for a movement such as BLM or call it inherently racist, please ignore this ignorance that is at the foundation of needing the cause in the first place. Please do not engage with the idiot. It is not racist to want to bolster your

48

subrace that has been systematically and systemically oppressed and killed off for several centuries on this and many other soils. We must accept that racism is at the foundation of this movement. We would not be here if racism didn't exist. Duh! If there was no racism and BLM came about, then they would rightfully be called Black Supremacists—much like how white supremacy came about and serves absolutely zero purpose. Black people do not oppress White people in any way when we ask to not be treated like it is 1875. We want to be able to vote freely without being arrested for the nitpickiest of reasons. We would like to be able to get coffee without being chased out by police. We would like to be able to buy groceries for our household without being pulled over and detained in the process because we have a brake light out. We cannot possibly oppress White people in any way by doing these things. No one can. We should not be called racist because we are trying to raise up our people from under the racist boot of white supremacy. We are a very strong and resilient subrace and we want each other to remember this, considering everything that we deal with in this world. What is wrong with being strong and reminding people that we are humans that deserve being treated as such? It tickles me when white supremacists say they are oppressed by every other subrace because people of color are being recognized as human beings and gaining the human rights back we should have had in the first place. The fact that anti-BLM people are complaining because we are fighting for our right to breathe and be human beings shows who these "Christians" really are on the inside. How can you seriously complain about a Black or Brown human wanting to be treated equally as a White human? If you can answer this question with any answer other than silence, then you fall into this category of bad people. Why is it okay for our, or anyone's, places of worship to be burned or desecrated? There is no cogent response to this as no one is doing this to their places of worship because people of any color have better sense and more respect for God than these "Christians." We are all equal and supreme because we are God's creation with our Souls as tethers to Her. No color is greater than another and the whole lesson of BLM is to get people to understand this equilibrium. It is not racist to make this point. It *is* racist to refute it.

This idea of Black people being racist because of BLM is the equivalent of a plus-sized person with low self-esteem coming out of their shell, doing things to improve their self-image and regain the confidence that was lost due to social judgments, then shaming them for doing so. When did subrace-shaming, or any kind of shaming, become okay? It is a product of a primitive mindset and way of living. Not everyone or everything needs to be clubbed over its head for us to survive, especially if our actions are based on our own fears, insecurities or lack of understanding. There is enough land and there are enough resources for people to live abundantly without being denigrated, domineered, murdered and robbed.

Generally, humans are awesome, respect and love all other people, even when our freedoms as human beings are trodden on, and do not proactively judge any person by their subrace. Good humans can live in harmony with anyone because we do not emphasize subraces as the sole factor in whether a person should be treated as a human. Our Souls should be equally respected as gifts from God, just as bad actors' Souls are, as the equal respect they demand is still given. Black people should not have to beg and plead for our lives with callous people, while they are standing, armed with military-grade weapons, over us with hateful, murderous intent or us standing in front of any law enforcer of the oppressing subrace for committing crimes associated with survival that the oppressing subrace has made virtually impossible to do. Of course, we have genocide happening in parts of Africa and vicious crimes happening within our own community and subrace borders, but this international strife is a symptom of colonization, and a result of the extreme and widespread overarching racism between Africans/those of African descent and some Caucasians. Nonetheless, all of it is bad and are actions of low-vibrating human beings. I am not downgrading or excluding other people of color's plights with racism in their lands—particularly, caused by those of the Caucasian persuasion, or anyone for that matter, but I cannot address every single thing in this book. I am only addressing the relevant parts of my struggles with them as a person of African-Indian slave descent living in America. My people (those of any color that ride with us in solidarity included), if any person attempts to make you feel bad for wanting to be proud of being Black or supporting Black people in our struggles when the other subrace has been telling us for so long that our lives are worth less than nothing because of our skin color, or because you are Caucasian simply trying to educate others in your group of their racist ways, ignore them by all means. Their ignorance and stupidity are contagious.

"Most people would rather be certain they're miserable, than risk being happy."
~ Dr. Robert Anthony

People who judge complain and cry way too much about other people and what they do. Put that energy into a cause or making a difference in your community. I don't give a fuck what cause or what you do to positively give back. If you have all of this energy to whine about other people doing or not doing things, just shut the fuck up and do it. Give back! Maybe if we spent that energy on noteworthy causes—not causes that further tear us apart as fellow humans, we would be happier, healthier, and feel better about ourselves so that we will not feel the need to cry and complain all the damn time about the rest of the world. The loudest, most frequent crybabies are usually the ones who do the least to affect the world in a positive way. People nitpick just for the sake of it. Some people are so miserable that their life is not worth living if they do not have some nitpicking or refuting to habitually do. If your life is defined by making others miserable, taking away any glory or happiness from others, or anything similar, then you have more problems than not. People who judge are likely devoid of the very things they deflect onto others. There's no happiness in a chronic complainer or judge. Happiness and judgment can't exist together. Happy people do not complain, blame, or judge others for anything. We must do better as people who are in the same human race.

So, grow up and get out of these low-vibrating habits. Nobody likes a bitch. Life is about living and loving, not fighting and hating.

"Happiness cannot be traveled to, owned, earned, worn or consumed. Happiness is the spiritual experience of living every minute with love, grace, and gratitude."
~Denis Waitley

Jesus and Our Salvation

2 Corinthians 5:1-14, 14-21 MSG

For instance, we know that when these bodies of ours are taken down like tents and folded away, they will be replaced by resurrection bodies in heaven—God-made, not handmade—and we'll never have to relocate our "tents" again. Sometimes we can hardly wait to move—and so we cry out in frustration. Compared to what's coming, living conditions around here seem like a stopover in an unfurnished shack, and we're tired of it! We've been given a glimpse of the real thing, our true home, our resurrection bodies! The Spirit of God whets our appetite by giving us a taste of what's ahead. He puts a little of heaven in our hearts so that we'll never settle for less. That's why we live with such good cheer. You won't see us drooping our heads or dragging our feet! Cramped conditions here don't get us down. They only remind us of the spacious living conditions ahead. It's what we trust in but don't yet see that keeps us going. Do you suppose a few ruts in the road or rocks in the path are going to stop us? When the time comes, we'll be plenty ready to exchange exile for homecoming. But neither exile nor homecoming is the main thing. Cheerfully pleasing God is the main thing, and that's what we aim to do, regardless of our conditions. Sooner or later we'll all have to face God, regardless of our conditions. We will appear before Christ and take what's coming to us as a result of our actions, either good or bad. That keeps us vigilant, you can be sure. It's no light thing to know that we'll all one day stand in that place of Judgment. That's why we work urgently with everyone we meet to get them ready to face God. God alone knows how well we do this, but I hope you realize how much and deeply we care. We're not saying this to make ourselves look good to you. We just thought it would make you feel good, proud even, that we're on your side and not just nice to your face as so many people are. If I acted crazy, I did it for God; if I acted overly serious, I did it for you. Christ's love has moved me to such extremes. His love has the first and last word in everything we do. Our firm decision is to work from this focused center: One man died for everyone. That puts everyone in the same boat. He included everyone in his death so that everyone could also be included in his life, a resurrection life, a far better life than people ever lived on their own. Because of this decision we don't evaluate people by what they have or how they look. We looked at the Messiah that way once and got it all wrong, as you know. We certainly don't look at him that way anymore. Now we look inside, and what we see is that anyone united with the Messiah gets a fresh start, is created new. The old life is gone; a new life burgeons! Look at it! All this comes from the God who settled the relationship between us and him, and then called us to settle our relationships with each other. God put the world square with himself through the Messiah, giving the world a fresh start by offering forgiveness of sins. God has given us the task of telling everyone what he is doing. We're Christ's representatives. God uses us to persuade men and women to drop their differences and enter into God's work of making things right between them.

We're speaking for Christ himself now: Become friends with God; he's already a friend with you. How? you ask. In Christ. God put the wrong on him who never did anything wrong, so we could be put right with God.

There is much confusion on Jesus's role in our lives today, but for the sake of keeping this message succinct but clear, we will just talk about what is popularly—though erroneously—known. Jesus's name generally means "salvation" with Christ meaning, "anointed one." His Passion (which, in Latin, dually means to endure or suffer *and* patience) is representative of the trials we endure in our human life and the healing thereafter, or resurrection and separation from the Karmic cycle. We suffer, and in this suffering, we find salvation, and our Souls are resurrected in a new form. We resurrect in the fullness of God's Divine Love. The cross, albeit older and in more universal variations in many other belief systems before being adopted by Christians as their symbol, is representative of the four corners or cardinal directions and many other things; it is symbolic of various parts of life, nonetheless. Jesus's resurrection is especially representative of our innate ability to overcome these trials if we relinquish everything and lay all of our troubles at God's feet, having immovable faith; thus, getting ever closer to Nirvana.

The more we shed of these heavy earthly things, the higher we begin to vibrate and the lighter we become. Our Souls are made of light. Our bodies are made of earth, or material. We are here to condition our Souls for beyond the "material." We are born with all the tools we need to overcome anything at any moment in our lives, no matter how severe. We just have convinced ourselves, in an unforgivable blasphemous insult to

56

Her, that God made inferior beings and refuse to see the lies or misinformation that were created and pushed over time to keep us in this low belief. Jesus died in the material form to show us that we can overcome anything if we shed these earthly delusions; although his actual physical death is still a matter for debate. In spiritual terms, in the death of his ego, or transcendence, he elevated to Nirvana. The meaning and path are more detailed than this, but it is the gist of Jesus's ascension above earthly things and returning the Soul to its rightful position, as God wants for us all to return to Her bosom full of love. The same for other Prophets that have come to help humankind understand this core principle. When we are separate from God, we have all of the heaviness of suffering and continual tribulations until we return. Think of any parent loving and protecting their child, but the clueless child decides to run away because they think they are grown, know everything, and can do better. The end result is always the same. The child learns the hard way that they do not know everything and needs to return home to learn through faith and trust that the parent knows what is best. For you Catholics out there, I am not apologizing for pissing on your parade but the Pontiff's position is also a self-appointed joke. God did not choose for anyone to represent Her down here in this fashion and I am sure this is not what Jesus had in mind with Peter and the church he wanted to carry on his messages. God is the One and Only. She has Her appointees, like Jesus and similar prophets, to get the Word out, but *no human* is a true liaison that speaks on Her behalf and can direct the world on what is right and wrong. For those wanting to argue this point, we shall start at what God thinks about Her representatives position on molestation and pedophilia. No offense to Pope Francis because he has been instrumental in the change of some of the world views on homosexuality and love in recent years.

57

He's awesome as a person! But, the Catholic Church itself has to go. It wouldn't be so bad if it wasn't preaching and teaching the wrong moral things—like chauvinism or intolerance, that gave birth to the backwards ideologies that are enforced in the world today, as people are free to learn the *right* things about God and our human duties, however they choose.

All of this is part of the lie that the Bible speaks about regarding Satan, the deceiver. Satans are high level demons and the Devil, or Lucifer and many other names, is allegedly the highest ranking one in many pagan beliefs but in Abrahamic and Christian tradition, the meanings are synonymous and refer only to el jefe—not his minions we call demons, or sometimes, daemons. In this case, it is the mass misrepresentation and misunderstanding of the Devil and satans' actual purpose in getting humankind so off-track that we have no choice but to return to God by using the church system itself. Let us never forget how the Mormon Church had $100 billion chilling in its coffers. Yes, that is a 'b' and, yes, I am talking about a church that is supposed to help the poor and those who seek refuge. The premise of having a place to congregate was religiously and spiritually purposeful, until that purpose turned into a judgment and profiting practice in so many of the mainstream sectors. People contribute to and worship in these places and are taught to judge others who respect and worship God in other places and in other ways. I am so confused by this. So, a church that uses charity as its cover to siphon the coins from their parishioners' change purses and all their other wrongdoings is swept under the rug, but males, specifically African Americans, who are fined for wearing their pants off their asses is an abomination? I don't want to see any stranger's uninvited ass crack but I use this example to illustrate the world we live in and what our true religious and social beliefs are. Just like my points on what goes on in the lives of LGBT+ people, we may not want to see it if it is against our beliefs, but it is not up to us to advocate for laws against it. We did not buy their pants nor should we tell anyone how to wear them. We have to stop trying to control other people's free lives, saying it is in the name of religion or what Jesus would do. He would not want us persecuting people because they are different. If you believe this, you cannot possibly believe in God and what Jesus was trying to preach because to denigrate others for who they are is to deny and disrespect the part of God that exists in us all. We should be adamantly using that energy to hold leaders accountable for their behavior and roles in all the grievances we have that make up all of our societal ills. It is all backwards, and we need to wake up to the many truths in order to save ourselves—our Souls.

Jesus, Muhammad, Buddha, and many others were all seen as the "Enlightened" ones because they understood the principle of suffering and the Soul's evolution as being our saving grace. Jesus was simply used as an overarching real-life example to the world that humans and their Souls have to suffer in order to rise above through strength and complete faith in God and our Higher Self in order to be saved. Jesus was not sent here as Her special "Son." We are all Her special "sons," or children, rather. Why the masses are not questioning the reputability of this truth yet require someone to submit a complete bibliography with a tweet or other social media post as etiquette, I will never understand. If Jesus allegedly died for our sins, why the hell is mankind and the entire world still so fucked up? Isn't this what he was supposed to have died for? Wake up, people! Use your own minds and do your own deep research to find the real truth. As another reminder, the Bible—the very same book that some people cowardly hide their bigoted and inconsistent beliefs behind—says those who seek the truth will find it. As it stands, people have been unreservedly believing anything that has been defecated out of these deceiving biblical translators' asses centuries before and continues to be perpetuated now, almost by force as the Romans did pre-Constantine. I will go deeper into this in subsequent media for those who are interested. But, people should begin their own research sooner than later to understand who Jesus really was as a person, not the deified version.

Another greatly misunderstood point is that Jesus did not want to be worshipped *as* God and that God is the only "good and true." There is only duality in God and Her creations (humans, plants, animals, the cosmos, etc.). Jesus is not a euphemism for Source or replacement when it serves someone's point or purpose. The trinity concept of being is referenced as Father-Son-Holy Spirit. The true trinity is the God-self: mind (conscious), body (physical), and soul (superconscious). Although these phrases and principles are synonymous and somewhat interchangeable, it still puts in the mind that the "Son" is the Jesus part of God, when this is actually all of us in the physical, which eventually dies away while the Soul is everlasting. This is the baseline premise of the idea of Jesus's story until it was mangled to the unfortunate mess that it is today. All of this is still God's omnipresence and benevolence in all of creation. Many Bible thumpers also dispute this in their blind, self-serving views, not open to learning more or realizing it is essentially the same thing but misleading and misrepresented, as already mentioned. Even Helen Keller could see that Jesus being the same entity as God is an area of great question (as many parts of the Bible, especially where the original smoking gun lies in books that were purposely left out of the printed/written canon)

60

when there are areas where Jesus refers to God as the *only* God to be worshipped, and referring to God in the third "Person," confirming Jesus is *not* God by his own admission. The most common example is Matthew 4:10, where Jesus tells Satan that he shall only serve the one true God. Jesus did not say you worship God *and* me homie; nor did Jesus *ever* definitively say he *is* God. Even the great archangels rebuked any worship, saying they are servants, just like us, unto the Source—God, Her/Himself. You and Jesus are one and the same. Jesus and I are one and the same. We are all mankind in the flesh, all here to do the Will of, have complete faith in, and solely worship the One True Creator all around us and in the Heavens. God resides in all of us in the form of love. This is the basis of Jesus's teachings. When we act like Jesus using everything he taught us and in releasing our God-love into the world through our actions; thus, becoming Christ. The act of helping and loving one another unconditionally is godly. We cannot worship a person who was ever in the flesh at any point in time just because they did their internal work and elevated themselves higher in Soul/Spirit. Jesus didn't come into the person he was until the years before his death. He was a normal bad ass kid and a normal working adult. We all can elevate ourselves to the light beings that we originally were, but every day, we choose not to live in that higher place of being. I have had this conversation with pastors of many churches who believe that Jesus is the One True God. Really? Ask God what She thinks about idolatry with Her people worshipping a human being idol. Jesus is to be respected for his ministry and who he was as a person, no doubt, but not worshipped. It seems a lot of Christians, especially those who have taken the position to "teach" the Word, are breaking the First and Second Commandment every second they hold these beliefs and pass them along to others. There isn't a gray area with the idea that some special detached part of God was sent down here for us to worship so we can explain away or give reason to our blind faith, or lack thereof, just to shut us the fuck up. This is a fabricated storyline that people over the centuries have been suckered into for a much grander purpose.

People will kill other people who challenge these beliefs because it forces them to see the truth, which people, naturally, are averse to—which is also backward, like the rest of this reality. People have always held their beliefs close because it answers what life is for them. Otherwise, they will be forced to have faith in something that is in no way tangible (though we see evidence of faith every day when the sun rises and in Mother Nature), and very few humans are strong enough to completely submit to that. It is the same fear that people have when challenged to give their last dollar to a homeless person, or run along with the idea that they must hold on to that last dollar because they do not know where their next dollar will come from—empowering fear and lacking faith that God will provide their next dollar as She always has. How do they think they got that dollar in the first place, and the dollar before that? We're always taken care of. We just aren't grateful enough to even recognize and give thanks for the most important blessings in life—like, food and shelter that, although may be a struggle for some, they always seem to have. When you have these things and someone else doesn't, reach back and help pull them forward as best as you can. Never selfishly watch your brother or sister struggle if you can help, even just a little. This could be from helping a coworker with their performance to doing an old nemesis a solid. We're all here to help one another in this life, and to soulfully grow from those experiences.

Changing beliefs involuntarily, in itself, scares the shit out of most, finding out the whole belief system they've built their entire lives on is false. That is the problem we have had since we discovered our ego-fueled free will in the Garden...why should we worship something we cannot see? That was clear evidence then and a symptom of evolution into the truly faithless humankind we are now that thinks it knows better than God. Misunderstanding who Jesus is is *the* sole reason humankind is here because we have looked to and praised something external to save our Souls when it is solely up to us to meet God all the way through our own redemption. Jesus's purpose was to lead us *back* to God and complete faith in Her because we lost our way for the fact that She is not tangible—we could not see or touch Her. We are to only worship God, not Jesus. We are not to blaspheme and call him God and worship the "main" God when it's convenient. We only fervently worship Jesus because we know he actually existed as a person; yet, when he was resurrected from the dead, we believed he still existed because we knew he was human at one point—similar to our knowledge that a passed on loved one still exists in the Spirit. Still, another example of our backward thinking just to appease and support our own insecure, heathen ways. Why can we not believe we were in the Spirit first and still very much connected to Source while in the flesh? What an absolute insult to our Creator! Then, we have the audacity to ask God why the hell are we suffering. We have affronted God well over these past 2000-plus years with this belief that a man was brought here to act on God's behalf, so we are totally where we deserve to be as humans; not that he was the first idol that humans believed in and worshipped. Would you continue to be there for people who constantly doubt your presence and efficacy...that you should only be called on when it is convenient because you haven't proved yourself the way they

63

wanted you to? God is always there and listening; we just don't like the feedback we receive when She responds. This is when Source gets ignored and Her existence called into question.

Jesus, or salvation, is in all of us to achieve, and it is our job to activate this energy and way of being in order to receive eternal life. If we do not, there is no way our Souls can reap the benefits of paradise on earth and in the afterlife. Jesus said in order to understand God and how we can reach Her, we have to act *through*, or as, him—i.e., his methods, acting as Jesus did in his treatment of others, activating our innate strengths and following his teachings to the letter. No random person can access a highly secured vault. The person will have to have an equal or higher-level security clearance or other extraordinary credentials to do so. This is no different. God's door is always open to us, but we will never be able to understand Her, Logos, and the meaning of all life if we are not fully in a non-ego state and do not come to Her correct. This is the principle of it all. You cannot vibrate low and expect high vibrating things to come your way or open up for you. Vibrations are like magnets; whatever level you are vibrating at, the Universe can only send you what your magnet's strength is attracting or pulling in. Thus, the law of attraction is if you are vibrating low (weak magnet), you will only receive (attract) low-vibrating things like strife, troubles, toxic people, etc. If you are vibrating high, you will be able to receive your heart's desires at that level of vibration—even increasing the level of vibration much higher in some cases. Whatever or wherever your vibration level, the Universe obliges, but it cannot give you what you are not ready for. This is the foundation of the law of attraction in full action. The Universe is all about what is right *at* the individual level for the sake of the whole *outside* of the individual, later to affect the rest of humanity. If you are unsure of what this means, look at your own life. Are you vibrating at a level where you are receiving your heart's desires and gifts commensurate with your vibration level, or are you vibrating low and wondering why you only receive heartache, pain, and people who only drain you and not any of the desires of your heart? We are put here to help humanity, and when we are not vibrating high, we are not fully connected to our Higher Selves to do the job we were put here to do. The thing is, people have total control over how their lives turn out. I often hear dissent to this thought, but it always comes from people who are full of anxiety, stress, and their life is full of misery and problems. People *choose* to be abundant and happy or to be miserable and wallow in it. The choice has always been ours until this thing called ego developed in humanity when greed became the ultimate way. We are the weavers of our own webs!

People of other beliefs are usually criticized—sometimes, ad hominem—by these so-called Christians when these others worship something else not called "God," per se. They are deemed pagan or heathens despite the meaning being the same for Source. Even I receive backlash for not using the word "God" and told that any other word used is blasphemous. I usually laugh at their ignorance and tell them to have a good day. However, these other belief systems are doing *exactly* what "Christians" do, and most of them existed before Christianity came into existence. Take the Ancient Egyptians, for example. They worshipped Ra, who was considered the God of all creation, with Horus being deemed the "Holy Child" like Jesus. There were various other deities they worshipped, for death, fertility, nature, the oceans, and many more. The Ancient Egyptians did all things in service of Ra, with every other deity coming in second to him. Do we not have a Mother Nature that we refer to for all things happening in nature? Do we not have Saints, like Joseph or Mary, that people pray to for various things or celebrated on certain dates? Do we not have stories of angels that some pray to for guidance and protection, or a reverence for the Angel of Death? Are they not worshipping the one true God and have their deities for special situations based on their knowledge at such an early era in humanity? So, how are we to deem Ancient Egyptian culture, or any other similar culture, pagan just because they do not falsely worship Jesus or maintain the main world religions' view of God in their beliefs? Who are we to ostracize them as (sometimes negatively) different or make that judgment on them when they are practicing in the same way as westerners in their beliefs? To answer these questions, please refer back to the *Judgment* section of this book. I don't care how anyone worships God and honors Her Logos, as long as they do.

The very first commandment clearly says we are to worship only one God and no other Gods before Her. Yet, we still stupidly follow what was set in motion in antiquity. I will never understand how people cannot see the clear writings on the wall regarding who Jesus really was, and even after this knowledge has been revealed to them over time, they still follow behind everyone else believing in something wholly untrue, damning their souls in the process. It's like joining a bunch of lemmings to jump off a cliff simply because the other lemmings are doing it, while the suicidal lemmings humiliate and judge the lemmings with common sense who do not plunge to their deaths. These are also some of the people who make the most important decisions for us in the world. They lead people off of cliffs for their own selfish purposes. We must allow only God and inner balance to be our only compasses.

We have to be able to do our own internal work. We should not be following these false "prophets" out here that are leading us down rabbit holes because we are so desperate to find salvation outside of ourselves or something to believe in if we are empty inside. It needs to finally be understood that: #1. Jesus himself is not returning, especially as the Messiah; #2. the Messiah does *not* have to be a man; #3. God created us with everything we need innately to resurrect from our suffering stronger and more faithful in Her to receive our place in Paradise. The amounts of followers these people amass are alarming. There is nothing wrong with being fans of people who can positively help us find our way and actually lead us to salvation, as this is what teachers do, but don't be a lemming and follow them off of a cliff if they are teaching more backward ideas for their misinformed benefit or profit. They should also not be worshipped or used as a replacement for our own internal work. Because this is prevalent all over the world, it is clear evidence that there is an enormous need for true spiritual guidance. People just follow anyone that says they can lead them to salvation. No matter what, we still have to do the individual work ourselves, and having guidance should not ever derail us or replace the need for our own internal efforts. Sergei "Vissarion" Torop is one of the latest examples of this. People worshipped him as if he was Jesus for almost three decades, even though he told them that he was not Jesus but his reincarnation. He lived with some of his followers in a commune and lived by actions drawn from Christianity and Jesus's work. However, as with most cults, there was an element of using fear and physical harm to progress his message by saying that only his followers would be saved during the apocalypse, so they had to do (and they did!) whatever he told them to do. Vissarion, collectively, had upwards of ten thousand followers (four thousand in the settlement and six thousand more around the world).

The world as we know it is coming to an end. Not the end of the world per se, but the end of this age. The Universe is resetting. Old things are dying and falling away, and we are coming back to God. The evils in and of the Universe are fighting as we fought in the apocalypse in previous cycles. Remember, time is not the same on earth as it is in the vast expanse of the Universe. The battle does not happen in a short time. It is continual. The battle has been going on forever, but it is coming to its apex, which is the apocalypse as it relates to this current life of humanity. Evil is pulling out all the stops because more people are fastly awakening, returning to our original state of peace within. We are returning to the "I am." To balance. Jesus gave us the blueprint for all of this. We need to study him and his words to understand; not all the words verbatim, but his messages in his words and decipher them as they pertain to life today. Remember, those of antiquity used their words in terms they would be able to understand at that time. Words and their definitions have changed over millennia, and we must account for this to fully comprehend the real underlying messages in Jesus's teachings and God's Logos. We have been doing it wrong because we were advised wrong through time. The resurrection is the rise we, as Souls, meet on earth to come back to God. God and I are one. You and God are one. This knowledge is seeing God, and seeing God is having this knowledge. Once we see God, we lose all ego and understand that God is all and all is God. Not seeing God visually but seeing God and understanding God and life, all through our Souls. Once we shed all of our earthly learned ways of thinking after this experience, we never return to our old ways. It is impossible to know God and to have seen Her then return to

68

not knowing Her. It is like experiencing pure happiness then wanting to go back to being empty. I have never experienced anyone being fully happy, then saying they didn't like it and want to go back to being miserable. All that is pure is priceless. Being empty is to be devoid of knowing and seeing God. It is an experience that completely fills us, and in that, there is no room for fear, loneliness, or sorrow. This is part of the foundation that Jesus was simply trying to establish within us when he taught us that everything we need surrounds each of us as Source provides but *starts* from within.

We are one in unity and one in the "I am." Understand what this is. Knowing God is seeing God. We can only understand the "I am" when we see and know (which is one and the same) God. As Neville Goddard said in many of his lectures, "being pure of heart is not the condition, but it is the consequence." We do not work to be pure in heart. We become pure in heart after we have seen God, when we have reached salvation. She will reveal Herself to us, and thus, we *gain* purity of heart. This experience will come different to everyone but will feel the same—inexplicably heavenly. We do not constantly work on ourselves to become pure of heart because any tooling we do to recreate this purity is earthly; we obtain pure hearts through the experience of knowing God. We maintain pure hearts through our humane work and in how we treat others. Listen to many of Neville's teachings about our connection to Source. It explains so much. We must not take the Bible literally as it was written in their knowledge and terms of that time. We must understand the messages, not take the literal meaning of them as many messages are encoded in the scriptures. It is up to us to learn the true language to understand the messages God has sent forth for us to grow and live as She intended for Her and our greater purpose. When one is ready, God will reveal Herself to them. And, only in that instance will you truly know God and see God—not before.

"Study to shew thyself approved unto God, a workman that needeth not be ashamed, rightly dividing the word of truth."
~ 2 Timothy 2:15 KJV
Read 2 Timothy Chapter 2 MSG

Matriarchy

"If you want something said, ask a man; if you want something done, ask a woman."
~Margaret Thatcher

Since the beginning of time, as pieces of a fabricated historical storyline has taught us, women were automatically painted in a malicious light or secondary positions. Lilith, Adam's first wife, is deemed a demon succubus because she demanded he treat her equally. She was created the same as Adam was. Lilith would be considered akin to one of the major players in the suffragette movement, such as African-American suffragists Frances Ellen Watkins Harper or Mary Ann Shadd Cary, or for those who have no intention of learning Black History, Susan B. or the Notorious RBG of our time. Lilith demanded equality. She demanded to be treated as a human, not as an object only for Adam's enjoyment. God created women as equal counterparts to men, with each of us having our special traits to share with one another. Women who stand up for equality or, otherwise, exhibit outspoken voices and temerity in the fight for equity have always been vilified. Black women experience this every day when we do not accept whatever is given to us. We were seen as promiscuous and uneducated to now being viewed as angry bitches when being Black in America and deemed angry is what makes us angry. It is like poking a bear when it is sleeping, then appalled when it reacts in a way one does not like. We are stereotypically judged at every corner of our lives. We are firm in ourselves and in our continual fight to be awarded the same natural opportunities to be successful, contributing parts of humanity as God created us all to be. Just like Lilith. We will not beg for anyone to like us because we exist. We will continue on in our fight because we are not the weak simpletons the same society of people who thought slavery and the experimentation, killing, and raping of us was humane wanted us to remain viewed as. That is all I will say about us.

Mary Magdalene was also viewed as a whore because the majority of her company were men, when she was, in pure fact, a devout follower of Jesus, one of his disciples, and a supportive intimate partner to him. It is in many writings that men did not believe in the strength of or want to listen to a female teacher, just like men dislike being under women in subservient work positions or even in the Catholic church today. Albeit, there are changes in the latter but there is still much fighting to be done for equality in positions in the Catholic church. Mary Magdalene was steadfast in her devotion to Jesus and spreading his teachings, even in his earthly death. If she was alive in this era, she would be equivalent to the many women who cross misogynist boundaries established in male-dominated industries and positions historically designated for only males to hold; albeit, those boundaries are not written anywhere as rules. For the longest time, women could not hold positions of power in business, government/law, or religion. They were reserved only for men. Even the papacy only favored men in these positions of religious authority—primarily as a measure to be able to influence and maintain omnipresent control over people's beliefs and morals (and everything else), but this is another conversation.

"It took me quite a long time to develop a voice, and now that I have it, I am not going to be silent."
~ Madeleine Albright

Women were kept out of everything, especially politics, so corruption could prevail. Compassion and nurturing are intrinsic in women. We naturally do not possess the propensity to allow any kind of suffering. We don't have the mind to allow or create wars, killing innocent people to prove a point, shrugging off these lives as collateral damage, or coming with the territory of world dominance/domination, unless these things are learned. When dealing with human beings' souls, we have to consider each one as equally important as the lives of the people making these inane decisions to continue to be biased against women or to cause war. It requires the ability to unconditionally love, which is not the easiest thing for men to do naturally. There is never any justification for war, but there is always justification for unconditional love. If we need to implement global policies regarding tyrant regimes, there are ways of doing it without affecting the human security of the constituents of these nations. Women have and will play the biggest role in returning the world to a heart-centered plane of existence. It is up to us to restore this since we've been forcibly kept out of creating this world when we are the ones who bring life into it. Our positions were manufactured as subservient; God didn't put us second to men. We were created equal in position to our male counterparts, not "less than," nor did we joyously elevate them to their position. We had no say in our destinies. Acknowledging the feminine is the hardest part of the masculine journey. This is why boys are told they are weak when they cry or love when they should be embracing these parts of their feminine sides to make them stronger and complete. This is why males struggle the most with their sexuality and have harder times expressing any sexual feelings, especially homosexual feelings of any sort. The patriarchy had to actively suppress women in every way, even the feminine in men, in order to climb to this ridiculous stature. Our actions, thoughts, the way we dress, and even when and how we have children were all controlled by men; even now, we still fight to protect the Roe v. Wade decision made decades ago. Anything to keep us in a subservient position will continue to be a thorn in society. We were not created to be objects to men. If God wanted us to be objects or in the position the patriarchy deemed us only valuable in, then I am one hundred percent sure we wouldn't have been initially created equal with thinking brains, capacities, and voices. Men are not above us, nor we above them. It genuinely is about equality in every form and respecting each other's gifts and strengths to the world. Just because a woman bleeds every month doesn't mean they should be paid less money to do the same job or are incapable of doing that job. Yes, there are some jobs that women may have difficulty physically doing, like jobs that require heavy lifting or immense physical strength, but it does not mean that we cannot try to do these jobs or that we should be paid less to do them. It should be up to the female applicant to decide what they physically cannot handle. No one should be telling another person what they can and cannot do in any capacity. It is *not* up to men to decide what we do with our bodies or control when we procreate, and it is insane to have laws regarding such. The patriarchy, in effect, isn't allowing duality in humanity to flow, hence the equality problems we see in the world as well as many of the other global issues we face. There are obviously many things that impact the state of the world. Allowing duality to flow in its many forms is the precursor to peace. If one part of something is suppressed, the entire lot is affected. This is not male-bashing before those crybabies come out of the woodwork; this is simply stated truth, just like reminding people why there is a BLM movement. We are all equal, and that is the bottom line—no matter color, sex, or preference. It is quite embarrassing and sad that some people have to be reminded of this in the 21st century.

Women are very powerful beings. We can bear children and have the strength to endure intense pain in childbirth and from the gift and curse of being blessed with the ability to feel. We are forced to be in lower positions in society, and we have acquiesced. We mentally develop faster than our male counterparts which helps us see our positions in the world and its pains earlier than we would like to. And, we love like no other. There were many female mythological goddesses across many cultures, and most were revered. Isis, Bast, Hera, Artemis, Durga, and many more were more powerful than most of the male gods, and highly respected and worshipped. Women are valuable to the world, and we just want our equal positions as God intended. No one has the right to take that away from us, just like no one had the right to treat living Black women like live lab rats during slavery to understand the female human body. Every human female should be treated as fellow humankind, not as objects. If you are a man with a daughter, how do you want her to be treated? Whistled at while walking down the street and called all types of slurs when she ignores this behavior? Raped and thrown away? Her ass slapped every time she walks by a guy?

Completely unhappy in her marriage because her husband says she is only his cook and baby machine? Doing the work of all the men at her job but paid less and never promoted? If Mary existed in her same divine position today, would all men treat her like every other woman is treated—abused, told she is only useful in the kitchen and sack, treated like an object all of her life and paid less? Would men change if she told them not to treat women this way anymore because it is wrong? What if this was how your mother was treated in the preceding decades? Are you going to do anything at all to help change this? Think about it, guys. It is not all about you anymore, and the reality is, it never was.

Pure Altruism and Humanity

We need to help each other channel the anger we have at society for the many things that it is plagued with into positive productivity, like making any kind of peaceful movement a conductive medium of exchanging ideas and expressing our grievances about the issue and its accompanying disadvantages to everyone. If we deny ourselves the soul-saving help we need as a whole race of people despite our differences, we are no better animals than the ones who created this world we now live in. It is so heartbreaking that the beautiful differences and individuality that God gave were turned against us. People who do not look like us, do not eat the same foods, who have different customs, or a different choice of sexual partner—whatever the beautiful difference is—has been used as a way to keep us unequal and of less value to others. That was not God's intention. She did not make us different so we can be targets of other people's aggression, insecurities, and other personal gripes. Our actions will fall in line with the images and stereotypes that already plague us. For example, Black people are treated like we are all violent, we are uneducated, and we do not know how to behave peacefully in any way. We do not need to give the opposition any more reasons to believe and feel that we are inferior to them in any way—which we are not and never will be inferior—and, as such, we are deserving of our right to breathe and love just like every other living, thinking thing.

Speaking to every human, no matter how we feel about people who have wronged us, we should not ever treat them badly or harm them in any way. This does nothing but increase our negative Karma jackpot. And at the rate people are going, it is about to pay out big time. Whatever you put out into the world is what you will receive. We must always, always, always follow the Golden Rule at all costs, in every way, no matter what. We cannot let fear and anger ever overcome us. We must be stronger than this. If you find your significant other cheating, do not run outside to key up their car and bust out their windows. If you do so, your stupid ass has just opened yourself up to negative Karma, and you won't like the consequences. If they cheated on you, roll out, quietly forgive them in your heart, and simply walk away. It is hard for many of us to "turn the other cheek," but we absolutely must. We all want to catch people who have wronged us in a dark alley with no witnesses and plenty of glass, but what does that do for our salvation? Will you feel good in the morning about that? Will you be able to cope with that for the rest of your life, let alone sleep that night? Walking away is God-like strength. People who are humble enough to do it are damn near saints because it takes great strength to not push someone into traffic or off an overpass onto an interstate. We have to be better humans. When we finally reach the point where people are no longer hurting people, we will no longer have these murderous urges when we are hurt. We will be more forgiving and energetically lighter because we are not holding on to the emotions of stress and anxiety that come along with harming another person materially or physically. Always be the bigger person and walk away. This does not make you weak but, rather, stronger than the person who harmed you.

Perhaps this part may fall under racism, but it very well falls under the area where there lacks altruism over profit. Most black and brown communities in the U.S. have an abundance of food deserts. These pockets of inhumane food insecurity should never exist. No human in this country, or anywhere, should be struggling to feed themselves. Food and shelter should never be on the list of things we have issues with, especially when we literally throw away more food than we consume. We have grocery stores with already razor-thin margins struggling to keep themselves in these communities. I am not talking about your nationwide chains (because you won't, or rarely, see them anywhere near low income, colored communities) nor your local Mom & Pop shops (or, corner stores as we call them in Baltimore) because they are usually one small store in the middle (or, on the corner) of a random neighborhood and usually do not exist to serve large communities of people. I am speaking of small local grocery stores that have opened their doors to fill in the gap that these large chains have left. There are communities of colored folks who cannot afford the higher prices of the larger chains, or they cannot get there. The only ones left in these communities after the local chains have shuttered due to their own income problems are corner stores and liquor stores. Do you see this in suburban communities? Hell no! As a matter of fact, corner stores are in shopping centers with an abundance of healthy food choices and are called convenience stores or marts—or, they just do not exist at all because of the existence of high-end stores the residents can afford. The corner stores in the 'hood are not convenient because they do not sell us items that are conducive to healthy living. How convenient is it to only be sold packaged goods full of fats, sugars, and chemicals with consistent consumption resulting in extremely poor health that will require the need for an already morally piss poor (or piss rich for those running or working in it, however you want to look at it) healthcare system? Poor health also affects the brain and behaviors of the consumer. It is common knowledge that a healthy diet is integral in any child's development, especially their brains. This applies to adults, too. Kids learn better and grow healthier on a stomach full of nutrients. They cannot learn shit with a brain full of fat and sugar; thereby, getting lower grades and some ending up lifelong offenders somewhere in the penal system or in low paying jobs, perpetuating our communities' wealth gap issues with both scenarios adding to the problem the major chains faced in the first place; perpetuating the cycle the chains can actually break (pun unintended although accurate and apropos). Of course, people will bitch saying this is a race card being pulled again, especially those outside of these communities who never have to worry about where their next fruit, vegetable, or whole meal will come from, or not even knowing food deserts are a real thing. *YOU* can have a whole broken glass seat...face first, Karen or Chad.

This issue is similar to redlining and works very well with it. If you have a corner or liquor store within one to three blocks in any direction from your home, you live in the 'hood. And, if you live in the hood, no real grocery or healthy food business will *ever* break ground there because of crime, low income, and the high ass price for shit that God put here for free; thus, resulting in food deserts. I am not sure about every other major urban area, but in Baltimore City, where I was born and raised, food deserts persist. There aren't any healthier food options offered by million or billion-dollar companies anywhere within a few mile radius, let alone one mile, to be considered a food desert in the first place. Many residents who already are struggling on a very low income (a good portion of them are seniors who are not ambulatory or cannot afford transportation) have to rely on the mercy of local food chains to bring sustenance to these neighborhoods. Still, they struggle to survive because of the very narrow profit margins. Even if these neighborhoods did have the major chains, they still would not survive because these communities cannot afford the higher prices. Most of these companies are too greedy to lower the pricing by even a penny to attempt to meet their constituents where they are. A penny isn't going to throw off their revenue in these neighborhoods. I cannot tell you how many times I have patronized stores in suburbia and paid less than I would at the exact same store in or near the hood. Also, many in the community have not even been exposed to or developed a taste for the healthier types of food because all they know is junk sold by uncaring corner store owners. Kudos to one multi-billion dollar national grocery store exception in addition to them bringing jobs to one of the roughest areas in our city. I will allow the goodness to exist in their action and not assume it is only because Johns Hopkins University is only blocks away on the other side of this area. The average corner store does not carry any fresh fruits or vegetables, and when they do, they are usually disgusting, old, or high priced. I have lost count of every corner store I have gone in with brown and moldy green peppers that crumble and smush when you pick it up to examine it. The eggs are four dollars for mediums. The cheese can be used as bricks in the new low-income housing developments. The canned goods are dented, expired, or swollen with botulism, covered in dust. However, they have candy, snacks, high fructose corn syrup, and blunt papers floor-to-ceiling and covering the windows that they sell out of almost every day. The liquor stores, same thing. Are they outlawed from carrying juice that doesn't have high fructose corn syrup to go with that malt liquor and $2 pint of vodka? Or, is it because we live such hard-ass lives that those things are foreign to us because we spend so much of our time trying to forget the lives we have been *forced* to live for the past several hundred years? Yes, forced. I doubt we would have proactively chosen this way of life if we had the freedom to do so. I am not in the military so I did not like being shot at every time I stepped foot outside.

During the holidays or natural disasters is when donations increase. There has always been the question of why large corporations destroy usable or edible items. Liability and profit are the two main reasons. As for liability of food donations, the corporations will be covered under the Good Samaritan Food Donation Act, which explicitly protects them unless they're out here purposely trying to poison populations of people. When asked why clothes are destroyed at designer clothing companies that are not recalled for dyes or other caustic chemicals, or otherwise contaminated, the reason is "so the items cannot be sold at discounted prices and sold to the 'wrong people,'" according to multiple news outlets. The practice's purpose is so that it retains its exclusivity. So, in other words, they don't want black or low-income, or both, people buying their shit and wearing their shit on the street as they lean. Creative directors don't want the affluent who make the occasional pass through the hood to get downtown to their lofts seeing designer colors/initials on a bus stop or leaning over or sleeping in a gutter; they'll stop buying if "these" are the types of people who wear them. There are ways of doing things, and this is not it. They care more about their images than clothing and feeding people. That is a problem, and it sadly stems from the buying habits of the affluent. What's wrong with repurposing last season's threads into usable pandemic masks and other medical PPE, donating them across the world under a subsidiary name? What about turning the material into tents or other types of small, weatherproof structures for those living in tent cities? Because saving people's lives is also apparently beneath them. I mean, look at the company who backpedaled using a monkey on their apparel with a little Black boy as the model to 'let's help those in poverty' using "similar" depictions and probably the same kid model. Don't think people didn't notice, you disgusting, racist dickbags. This also goes for companies that take African culture, put a "white" spin on it, and call it their own, or completely screw it up. If they're this culturally insensitive, why would we believe they'd help people struggling to survive but want to dress and feel nice sometimes, the people they employ in their stores at low wages, or those who suffer (or get killed, like in Bangladesh) in their sweatshops? These billion-dollar companies would rather stay billion-dollar "exclusive" rather than billion-dollar companies that become "exclusive" trillion-dollar companies that help people around the world. People buy more when they feel they are a part of something real, not a gimmick to donate a penny to some village that never sees it with 99 cents going toward the "handling" of the donations back into their coffers or into an adjacent offshore one. The greediest, yet the dumbest, shit I've ever seen. There are financially wealthy individuals who make these decisions, and just thinking about them makes my stomach turn as I envision them with faces like the lawyers in the movie, *Devil's Advocate*. How can they go through life and sleep peacefully, knowing their decisions affect the people they're not thinking of or purposely trying to avoid? The devil has no problem getting his eight hours clearly, but the people already struggling to survive have to pick up the slack for these greedy, ugly people on the inside. If more of the affluent held these executives accountable for their actions, they definitely wouldn't do it because it threatens their revenue. If they began to become bargain basement buys because of protests from the affluent against buying those brands, they'd scramble to revamp their entire image. No question because, obviously, most people with money don't care until being low-income or impoverished affects them personally.

I do not know what the hell the problem is (actually, I do!), but I know we are tired of the mistreatment and starvation because millionaires and billionaires cannot contribute to the problems they penultimately, well, ultimately, have caused (the creation of capitalism then perpetuating the distribution and separation of wealth—keeping us away from it by any means). It is now obvious that this belongs in the racism section, also. And, as one of the wealthiest countries in the world, there should never be one hungry person on this soil, unless they choose to be. Altruism applies to everyone to exhibit. We have seen the numbers. We know that one billionaire can *give* one-tenth of their wealth to local nonprofits fighting poverty, and it will be the equivalent to the value of the third yacht they just bought. One of many billionaires will cry about separating from $150M to go to a local nonprofit in the community their money comes from and that they are going to write-off on their taxes anyway but will slam ass spend $300M on a jet just to fly roundtrip from Miami to Philly for a steak and cheese. It seems the working people have to do what the conglomerates and all the governments should be doing since it seems that our government works the same as a business now. We have to help one another since these corporations and the billionaires we created with our patronage are too busy counting, hoarding, injecting, and snorting away their coins. Oh, wait, we still have to figure out the problem of racism in order to help *everyone* not starve because black people are not good enough to eat the fresh fucking fruits and veggies we tilled in the first damn place; we are *still* only allowed the "junk" foods and waste animal parts that massa wouldn't even eat himself. It is funny how we are always blamed for our problems—the "why are you hitting yourself" horseplay, except this isn't fun or funny. Some things we just cannot control. We all need everyone's help to help everyone. It is not about color. It is about humanity.

This is an example of how we do not care for each other within our immediate reach. Please stop using your cars to control other drivers by slamming on brakes just because someone is tailgating you. If they annoy you, move out of their way or let them go around you because, eventually, they will move over or get the picture and get out of your ass. Obviously, they have somewhere to be. Even if they don't, it's not your job to police them with a 1-2 ton weapon that's moving at higher than parking lot speeds. It is so very annoying when people impede all other traffic when the rest of the world is moving at a faster pace and you simultaneously have someone next to you or in your blind spot doing the same. However, you do not know who is next to the tailgater and maybe they are just trying to get over in front of that car to pass you. They aren't intentionally tailgating you in this case and possibly not even looking at you but in their side view mirror in that split second when you decide to slam on your brakes in trying to clear the car they are attempting to pass. You also don't know who is in the car w/ them. Having a multitude of family and close friends in the medical field as well as having worked in it myself for a brief stint, I have seen and constantly hear stories of people's loved ones, including improperly secured babies, being killed or severely injured by being thrown through windshields then run over by other moving traffic because of that dumb ass shit. You do not prove any points with this contemptible, immature action other than your own idiocy and your stupidity can and will cost someone their life—possibly your own, Lord forbid in any case. And, for what...what will you have proved in this situation other than exhibiting the ugly, selfish type of person you've proven yourself to be? How would you feel if this happened to your teenager, or your pregnant friend or spouse, or anyone you love? Think of everyone outside of yourself that is involved in the consequence of your brainless action. It's totally unnecessary and an utterly ridiculous thing to do. Get your shit together people.

Give of yourself, humans, even if it hurts. We have to care more for one another. This is the ultimate act of altruism and being like Jesus, who *never* let anyone starve. We have to treat each other as if the situation is ours to receive.

Don't Be a Dumb Ass All Your Life

I have come across people who are just stupid. Plain and simple. Not intellectually stupid, but they do dumb shit that makes zero sense, or they knowingly do stupid things that hurt themselves or other people "just because." *Just because* is only a good reason if it is for a positive purpose, such as sending someone flowers *just because* or telling someone they love another *just because*. An opposite example is watching a show of daredevil stunts, and the disclaimer pops up to tell us not to do the shit at home. Firstly, why are there people in existence that we have to have common sense mentioned before everything we do? Secondly, if a person is this stupid, why do we have to suffer to protect their dumbness?

No matter how many disclaimers a company puts out there, there will always be dumb asses trying to out-dumb themselves, and the company gets sued for the stupidity of these people. If you did not order a cold coffee, assume the shit is hot. If you brainlessly throw back a hot coffee, then you deserve your burns as a lesson to use your brain. I do not feel a company that sells hot coffee has to remind people that the coffee is hot. I am not talking about a situation where the temperature is unregulated and the coffee is hotter than the food industry's highest beverage temperature threshold (yet another disclaimer for the idiots who just feel the itch to say, "Well, what about…" Shut the fuck up!), or a cap popping off that was not properly secured by your barista as this happens sometimes with a lot going on in trying to grab the cup, put money away, grab our phones, keys, open the door to leave, etc. I am only speaking about pure idiocy. Another big, but multifaceted, example is a person knowing they are not supposed to drink or smoke because they have kidney or pulmonary problems, but they do it anyway *just because* they want to. However, when they have to be rushed to the hospital because they have stones, developed cirrhosis or have returning pulmonary embolisms, they want people to be by their side and sympathetic to their ailment. They are not suicidal, or at least they do not present this; they just love to drink or smoke, or happen to be around others who smoke or drink, and they have very little willpower to say no when a smoke or libation is offered. They are endangering their lives and disregarding those around them who have to suffer through watching them suffer and the reeling thoughts of the implications of their loss in the household, *just because*. Although it is their body and life, doing these things *just because* is not a satisfactory explanation when God supplied us with brains to think past the short-term happiness, or whatever, from these earthly temptations.

Some people's actions are really that damn brainless and/or the person is truly that weak where their weaknesses become stronger than their will to save their own God-given lives. They do not have the consequences front of mind, or just do not fully care (even though they may say they do) how it affects them or others that love them because they are only concerned with satisfying their wants at that time. That short time of satisfaction is greater to them than the long-term effects of the consequences. Being the person that I am, I always very bluntly tell these types of people to be more cognizant of their actions and remind them of the consequences they are already fully aware of—friends and strangers alike. I do not care who I offend with *their* truth because, obviously, they need to hear it. Does it make a difference to their stupidity? Of course not. For some, this example may fall under substance abuse, but generally, people who have redundant health concerns related to the very thing that contributed to the health issue in the first place should know better. Their doctors tell them they should know better, their body loudly tells them this shit, and their family and friends tell them they should know better, so why is it that they do not, or refuse to, know any better in these circumstances?

Listening is an essential aspect of this. In another corner of the same box stemming from the last point, some of these people have a maturity problem...they are not mature. What do most kids do when someone tells them not to do something? They do not listen and do it anyway, despite the reason behind them being told not to, because they want to do what they want to do. Funny story. God told Adam and Eve's ass don't touch shit on that tree...that tree over there called the tree of knowledge or wisdom. What did they do? They went ahead and ate the forbidden fruit anyway, listening to the wrong mofos. Seriously! God of all of...I don't know...everything, told them not to do something, and they did it anyway. They actually thought they knew better than Her. That was the point She was trying to make. We do not know better than Her, and we cannot dictate to Her, so we must suffer the consequences of not listening in defiance of direct orders. Governments, lawyers, and judges do not know better; psych doctors do not know better; no one knows anything about your Soul and its path except God and you. If we were in a world that started with *only* listening to Source's guidance instead of only knowledge of/from our own egos, our only shepherd today would be God—not ourselves, not the Joneses, not Instagram influencers, not scientists who force you to believe there is no God and that human ingenuity and technological innovations are the only things keeping the earth going. We would not need governments and its greedy puppets to tell us what to do to keep us in order, because we will not be disorderly. We would not be continuing to harm our environment, ourselves and other people, or steal from nations and their people, causing unnecessary wars, because malevolence wouldn't exist. We would not be constantly fighting each other because all of humanity would be taken care of and would want for absolutely nothing. There would be no urge to harm or steal from anyone else. As I said, greed has become "the way." Our tiny actions have collectively gone that deep, and this is the very meaning of our actions affecting others beyond six degrees. We do not know Her intentions and do not need to question what She tells us to do. Our only job is to shut the fuck up and do it, whatever *it* is.

This was the beginning of the development of the ego—challenging God and Her instructions. This is another reason why humanity is here in this position of despair. No one is great enough to challenge God, especially those in my example above who think tomorrow will always be there, while they enjoy that quick buzz that only lasts a few minutes. No one can think for another person that is over the age of eighteen. However, there are a few ten-year-olds I would trust with responsibility more than some forty-year-olds. My friends who act as my "nice" filter give excuses for these people, saying that there may be a reason for their actions as an attempt to nullify their scatterbrained decisions or by saying, "It is still their life. If they want to die, let

90

them." That is like saying nothing when you see someone at a gas station near a pump lighting a cigarette even though it is common knowledge and there are signs everywhere to not do this. So, does that mean I am to not do my job in helping them understand their actions better or watch them just blow up the whole damn block with people, including children, myself, and residences in the vicinity, just so they can take a quick relaxing puff that can wait until they are off the premises in 5 minutes? It is one thing to smoke *knowing* you are not supposed to, but you do not care because you are depressed and quite possibly suicidal, or even a momentary lapse in judgment that we all sometimes have. Those are another scenario altogether. But, if the person is *knowingly* endangering their life by *knowingly* furthering the damage to their health in full *knowing* of the consequences to themselves and the pain loved ones experience from constantly being in this situation with them, there is no justification for that other than the complete inaction of their cerebral brain cells and utter selfishness. Do *not* make excuses for these people. Their actions are selfish to themselves and those who love them, and since they are knowingly killing themselves, it is a stupid action. I am not speaking to suicidal people who need help in other ways. That is no laughing or stupid matter. I am only talking about those who are acting stupid—the foolish senselessness they employ on a continual basis. They seriously need to ask themselves why they are actively engaging in such behaviors and what those behaviors are satisfying. We cannot make excuses for these people because these excuses only fuel these inane actions and cause others further damage from one person's inability to think past the moment. I have watched this same type of person get mad when people who love them tell them to think about their actions and cut people off because of the lectures. I wonder if they react the same to the doctors in the ER or their PCP when they tell these chimney or fish people their actions will indiscriminately and quickly put them six feet under. Your life is more important than a fag or joint or a beer. Please stop being a dumb ass all your life and grow the fuck up! If these things help you escape the sadness of your life, read the *Faith and Happiness* chapter of this book so you can be happy and healthy again.

We create our own heartaches and pains. We create our own misery and suffering by not being mindful of everything, including the people that will, subsequently, be hurt by our decisions. Some things just cannot happen when we do not use our brains for something other than a cobweb-covered dust bowl. The same principle exists in loving and caring for ourselves properly; when we do not exercise self-care in all areas, we cannot possibly love and care for another properly. If we do not care for ourselves, how can we care for one another? It is paramount that we consider others in our stupid decisions because they ultimately affect more parties than the single selfish dick. This acts counterproductively to the Golden Rule, contrary to what one ignorantly thinks. Indeed, our lives are our lives to live or totally disregard just the same, but we must remember our theatrics always affect the lives of others. Get your shit together people—Zhen Shan Ren!

"Think of how stupid the average person is, and realize half of them are stupider than that."
~ George Carlin

Our Habits, Patterns, and Thoughts That Affect Our Mental Health

The biggest problem people have is maintaining healthy habits and thought patterns in their daily waking lives. We have become so consumed with what society tells us is right or "normal" (which is subjective in itself), wrong or the "in" thing to do that we have lost individuality and struggle with keeping up with things that are not necessarily what we need, want, or are supposed to do. For example, people may blindly follow a total idiotbox on social media and do everything this particular idiotbox says, no matter the imminent peril we are exposed to when we lose, or freely give away, our common sense or sense of self in trying to be one of the sheep. That makes absolutely no sense. Why would a perfectly imperfect individual, as God created each of us, want to be just like everyone else that is full of heartache and problems? Why is it so important to fit in? People are afraid to be themselves...people are afraid to be different. If we were all supposed to be the same, then there would be no differences between us whatsoever. This is a form of social control that is now on autopilot, mostly for profit. To properly execute and do our part in God's ultimate plan, we cannot make our own changes, changes we *think* are for the best. The best for whom? We are born precisely how we are needed to show up here on this plane of existence. Again, changing who we are innately is not our decision to make. We always fail to remember that all of our actions and thoughts affect the rest of humanity, so when we are not being who we are born to be, we are depriving the world of the gifts God gave us specifically for the world to have. Being disconnected from ourselves causes us undue grief and stress in trying to be someone else; hence, the uptick in mental health problems and substance abuse. People are literally trying to escape the false reality they created. No logic exists here.

"Instead of wondering when your next vacation is, maybe you should set up a life you don't need to escape from."
~Seth Godin

When we try to fit in or be like the rest of the sheep, we lose our individual identity. Thus, we are giving our freedom away by becoming slaves to a damaged society's whims. We aren't born full of these things, but instead, we have created our own anxieties, depression, and stress because of the demands societies have placed on people to be sheep so that they are easily controlled by the forces previously mentioned in this book. These are the same forces that do not want us to think freely because they, then, lose unwarranted control over us. More people than ever are coming forth because they suffer from mental health issues related to identity and self-efficacy, or the loss of such. We must eliminate our self-created woes, take charge and be who we are supposed to be, who we desire to be. If you feel that you are more comfortable in the body of the opposite sex, then so be it. Trying to be something that you feel you are not because society is telling you otherwise creates internal struggles and turmoil that

94

does not need to exist. What you do with your body is between you, God, and your genitals, not your genitals and the rest of the world. We already have enough to stress over on a daily basis in trying to maintain our own sanity without having to add what society wants from us to the heaviness.

We have to learn to operate fully from being in the moment of living our best lives and feeling the best about ourselves. We are not here to appease everyone outside of our personal selves. Even those in our personal lives need to understand that one needs to sometimes put themselves first in order to be a complete and fully functioning person for those outside of themselves. This is nothing short of self-care that we are entitled to. Anyone who does not understand this and support you when you take this time out for yourself is not someone you need in your corner at that time or going forward, no matter who they are to you. This even includes our closest loved ones, and it is okay to reevaluate their position in our lives. Some parts of society allude to us the belief that we are forcibly obligated to deal with family or other loved ones solely because they are who they are. If a parent is toxic to us, it is okay to separate ourselves from them in the healthiest way possible and not feel any regret in doing so. We have to remember they are fallible humans just like everyone else that we encounter in life, and we must, still, live our best lives regardless of who is in it. Enablers are toxic people, too. They do not support your growth if they are aiding you in continuing your bad habits. These are also people whose positions need to be evaluated no matter how well-meaning they may be. It is okay to talk to these people and tell them your needs. If you do not, it is a disservice to the relationship and yourself. Once you have made it clear what it is you need from them, it is their responsibility to either stand up to their commitment to you as their position entails or to stand aside to let you grow without any ill feelings towards you for doing so. It is important that the lines of communication always remain open with your support system, or they cannot fairly do their part. Trust, communication and honesty within that communication are the integral pieces to the solid foundation of any successful interpersonal relationship to generate healthy situational outcomes. I cannot stress enough in this book how important and multifaceted communication is.

Simultaneously, we are only here to do our part in humanity that is completely separate from what we do behind closed doors, which is no one's business. What we choose to do in our own private affairs has nothing to do with society, as long as we are not harming others in the process. If I am a highly effective grade school teacher, but I like to have wild adult sex parties, who gives a shit as long as none of my students are there slamming down Harvey Wallbangers behind my bar while they pass out the condoms. My stellar ability to teach and bring forth future leaders has absolutely nothing to do with anyone or anything except to the people swinging from my ceiling in studded leather underwear while learning that weight distribution is crucial to not breaking the harness. People who make it their life's work to share their judgmental misery are likely the same committee members who complained about the two brides kissing in the 2019 Christmas Zola ad on the Hallmark channel or the people who complained to General Mills about the interracial couple in the 2013 Cheerios commercial...2013, for fuck's sake, not 1813! The problem is that when we created this pseudo world in order to fit into what society wants or deems proper from antiquated ideas of what 'right' is, we ended up hurting others because we are not functioning from a place of higher being; thereby, we are not doing our necessary part in the undeniable interdependence that being human entails. I applaud the changes seen on tv with more interracial couples and children, LGBT+ people and those of use who are just different being shown as people, too. We are finally moving in the right direction, as it only took a few hundred years. All people are differently equal, and God loves it. Why don't white supremacists...why do they hate everyone else so much, saying it is God's Will when we are made in Her likeness? Do they hate God, too?

People who are not living as the people they desire to live as wind up with mental imbalances that the mind creates in order for living to be more tolerable, no matter what form that specific action takes. For example, these people become angry and abusive in various ways to others and self, as well as creating an unlivable environment for those around them; sometimes, causing the support system additional stress as well, exacerbating the issues they have to deal with in their own circumstances and increasing the number of people out here losing their minds to other people's actions. These ways of being are selfish to the individual and to the ones that love them; and, in some cases, even to complete strangers. People who work in retail deal with it constantly—someone comes in having a bad day, and the retail agent becomes that individual's punching bag. This agent then takes their frustration home and lets it out on everyone around them. The kids in the house are now affected and may become bullies at school, and/or the spouse will become suicidal, end up cheating for comfort, or start cutting or abusing substances to cope with the miserable household life they have to endure. This is why we have so many angry or anxious people existing—not fully living—on this earth. We simply just need to stop being so angry as individual people and a society, and taking our personal frustrations out on others that are completely extraneous to the situation. It really is that simple. If the agent is a loved one and someone did that to them, you would be furious. Why do the same standards not apply to others but only to our selfish asses and loved ones? Are they not important enough, or do we just not care about those separated from us by multiple degrees? In the latter situation, we must remember that our actions and potential outcomes still affect others' lives, even at a great relative or spatial distance. Another angle of this example is your kid goes to school with the agent's kid, and the agent's kid ends up bullying your kid or other kids because you were a dick to their parent, causing the last shoe to drop for the agent's spouse who then commits suicide because of the abuse stemming from your treatment of the agent that day. The kid is a bully now and grows up to be a murderous psychopath because of the resulting traumas other people caused. We never know anyone's situation, and everyone's energy, in any form, travels beyond the selfish pricks that we can be.

We have to change our thought processes. We have to get to a point where it is easy for us to accept who we are regardless of society saying it is not okay to be who we are, which, in itself, is asinine. It is perfectly okay to be who you truly are and want to be (I cannot reiterate this point enough—*as long as you are not harming anyone*). Who told you that it wasn't okay to be yourself? If the answer is anyone other than you, then your work now needs to be in working on your inner strength and sense of self because *no one* can tell you what to do with *your* life and who you are supposed to be. When people try to tell you that wanting to live as the opposite sex is an abomination to God, tell them to take a running jump and that is between you and God. Do not let these people deter you from whatever makes you happy because they are not. Happy people will never tell you what is right or wrong in *your* life as they know that only you can determine that. People that tell you otherwise do not understand what happiness is, have likely never experienced it in living their truth and/or simply do not possess happiness at all. We must always live out our passions because if they bring us joy then they come from a higher place that no one has judgment over. I know plenty of people who do not live their truths because they do not want to offend their religious parents, do not want to be judged by society or are confused by one or both of these things. People who truly love and support you will not allow you to live in misery, no matter what their own personal preferences or prejudices are. These things are theirs, not your to build your life around. We must know this as fact and create a mindset and life based on this fact.

"The power of imagination makes us infinite."
~ John Muir

If someone ever tells you it's okay to not be okay, do not listen to them. They're ultimately telling you it's okay to be depressed, weak, miserable, negative, and unhappy, and that these things are normal. Although no one should ever be ashamed of not being okay because *recognizing* one is not okay *is* okay (it is what pushes us to change for the better), we do not want people becoming complacent in their low vibrations by thinking that it is okay to not be okay and to stay that way. No, it's not, never was, and never will be okay to not be okay. We were not born *not* okay. We developed and normalized these *not* okay things by living a disconnected-from-God life that society made us live by teaching us and making us believe that this is *the way* to live and how life is supposed to be. Do you think Jesus was ever depressed other than his sadness for how humanity treats each other...do you think Gandhi or Mother Teresa was ever full of anxiety? Do you think Buddha was walking around like a zombie on antidepressants? Hell no! They had immense courage and strength and understood that these low-vibrating energies were not of God. It is never okay to accept lower energies not of God and making them a way of life. Accepting that you are bipolar or clinically depressed is a symptom of low vibration. It is not to be accepted as your way of life, no matter how much you have been convinced that you will never be okay. Is that what you want...to live the rest of your life depressed and sad and as a walking dead shell because you feel you cannot be happy? Once again, we are entitled to the gift of happiness, if you are vibrating low, how can you attract things that are high or have a full-on high vibrating, happy life? How can you wholeheartedly believe the words of someone who has the same mindset or unfulfilled life or someone whose livelihood is to make you believe that you can never be happy again over what God has promised us at humanity's dawn? You can be okay if you choose the path to being okay. It seems to be easier for humanity to believe that life is supposed to be miserable but ridiculously hard for people to accept pure happiness as their truth or love from another person that they deserve, or to even fully love themselves. Why is this? Why do we purposely shun the thought that we can be truly happy or unconditionally loved but easily accept the idea that we are undeserving of these heavenly gifts? Why do we fear happiness and love so much that we poison ourselves to keep those needed things from us for which their lack is what caused the imbalances in the first place?

Gandhi, Jesus and other high-vibrating people never said, "Go ahead and keep throwing man-made drugs at these issues; you'll find the right cocktail to magically make your mental health issues better to live with because they will never go away...you'll be fucked up forever." No, no, no! This is completely wrong, and the people that do this are the reason why these things still vastly exist. We end up with more problems than we began with—whether it's the side effects from the drugs or never reaching Nirvana because we have suppressed the push to get there by numbing ourselves. People put too much faith into these scientific drugs and the "peddlers" of them that only healthily maintain their own gainful employment and yacht purchases, while those in need of help still suffer. This is also why the establishment is hell-bent on banning drugs like marijuana and other psychedelics. They're natural God-created remedies that were used for thousands of years to help people *deal* with mental or mood problems, health problems, and even religious rituals, to "see" more clearly, and to think for themselves with an open mind. That was before people realized they were more helpful as always known to be but less lucrative than the junk pharmaceutical companies, along with the help of colluding "medical professionals" that cannot profit from natural remedies, need and want everyone to believe. A great majority of mental health issues related to mood can go away with the *right* therapy, faith in themselves, and increased faith and trust in God. Mental health problems related to emotions and mood need to be fixed the same way they arose, not by a pseudoscience that is still in its infancy. Things originating in the mind cannot be fixed by chemicals from a test tube or people who try to lump everyone in everyone else's boat. One person's issues are not the same as the next because each person's psyche/Soul is different.

Anything abused or overused can be bad for anyone, but when prescribed correctly, the natural remedies can be of much help to humanity's collective good. Even water can be detrimental if there is overconsumption, but we have guidelines on how much we should drink for it to be generally healthy for our bodies to benefit. Thank God, more doctors are realizing this about marijuana. More efficacy studies of the coca leaf, marijuana, opium, and other things found in mother nature need to be funded to find out how to better use what God put here for every single human malady as opposed to trying to play God or be better than Her by downplaying the actual benefits Her creations inherently possess in creating stigmas and things that almost always cause more ailments; thus, more healthcare and pharmaceutical profits. Any layperson can look at the side effects of marijuana in comparison to your everyday antianxiety, antidepressant, etc. Hell, all you have to do is turn on the tv to see a drug commercial when the list of the side effects they read off are at least twenty seconds of the thirty-second time slot. Nothing compares to or can outperform God's wonders and work. Why would anyone want to take something for depression that is going to possibly give them a stroke, cause all their hair to fall out, or exacerbate their suicidal thoughts all just so they can "deal" with their depression better instead of getting rid of it completely? I don't know about them, but, for example, I'd rather find the right strain of weed or another completely natural remedy that will uplift my mood and work with that remedy, alongside my cannabis doctor's or therapist's recommendation, to help me build my courage to work through my depression to completely end it. All of this while I keep my hair, not have to take extra meds to quell my urges to randomly jump off of a bridge or to lower my chances of stroking out at any time, on top of not having to take meds for the side effects those additional drugs will cause, and so on for those.

One of the problems I have seen in my own mental health treatment in the past is that they try to force people to believe that even though numerous traumatic experiences may cause anxiety, depression, and PTSD, only drugs would help one live better with it, but they would never be able to make these things go away. Why not, is my question? I have always been a firm believer in God and that anything I want to change can and will do so because of my faith in Her and my own tenacity. So, in my past mental health situation (and because I am a strong Leo), instead of believing these things, I was hell-bent on proving them wrong. I refused to live feeling like shit every single day. So, I opened my eyes (both from my mood and the drugs) and made it my own personal mission to get out of believing these greedy dicks who only believed in their textbook gods and human lab rats, not in the same God I believed in. Not only is something created in the mind fixable by the same, but I also did not need their drugs to do it. I went through so many different psychotropic drugs because nothing worked over time, except in increasing my rage, since no drug was going to heal what was wrong inside of me. Some of the meds that aren't mood (neurotransmitter) enhancers or the ones that completely put you in a coma are placebos anyway. The others alter your synapses in seeing things differently when we can just change our perspectives on our own. We either don't want to do the work or we prefer someone or something else to do it for us. Mind over matter has always been my main mantra.

"Change your thoughts and you change your world."

103

~Norman Vincent Peale

Psychology is the study of the psyche. The definition of a psyche is the human soul, mind, and spirit. How in the hell is something physical like a pill going to completely heal an ailment not physical in nature, especially when the problem is not physical or caused by something physical? Even when others stress us (as they are physical), it is the struggle with the emotions behind the situations with others and even other's own struggles with themselves (none of which are physical for you but are founded in the psyche) that cause our minds to alter, even chemically. When we are born, we are born as clean slates. We can either learn to return to where we were spiritually only a few short moments before birth or we can follow in everyone else's miserable footsteps. We can learn the good, or we can learn the bad. Our brains are more open to good, and that is why many children can see things that adults cannot. But, what do we do as adults to these children and later on as adults? We diagnose the children with ADD or ADHD and drug them, then they carry that habit into adulthood. We do not take the time to teach them about the things that may be causing their issue and putting them on a course to always rely on drugs to solve their life problems and how to deal with them internally.

As children, we knew that there was more out there. Our minds were open to imagination. Our imagination is our Soul speaking to and through us. We have invented ways of explaining away the unexplainable things we fear or do not fully understand. If babies could talk out of the womb, they would tell us all the secrets of the Universe and what our Soul's journey is so we would never have to do any work to grow from the lessons we are here to learn on our soul evolution pit stop. Think of how many times we may see a baby laughing or staring at something we do not see, like cats do? There is an old wives' tale that says God or angels told us secrets just before we were born and they placed a finger on our lips, saying 'shhh', thus creating our philtrums. Since my grandmother died when I was only eight years old, I have always been able to see people before they died or just before their souls moved on. She also only came to me when the messages pertained to my mother. As an example of being an imaginative child, I remember being no more than 9 or 10 years old, telling my aunt and mom that I saw a woman in the hallway the night before, and they told me it was my imagination in the general sense and it was nothing really there. Later that day, we got word that one of my other beloved aunts had transitioned. I wasn't a crazy kid with a vivid imagination. I had a gift that adults refused to see (later on, I found out they were hiding it from me) and did not help me understand it. It happened many times after that, even with my mom this year, but I daren't tell unawake people this. I'd be committed because of their own disconnection and lack of Soul knowledge. Everyone's psyche is vastly different from one in a textbook or someone experimented on in shock therapy fifty years prior. The beautiful gift from God to connect to the spiritual world cannot and should not ever be eradicated or walled up by man-made drugs that alter the brain's natural function so that it works in a way that the rest of society wants it to. People should also help children understand and hone their gifts, not tell them they are challenged or different in a bad way.

I needed to cleanse and heal myself and return back to knowing and understanding my gift. Mental health recovery is different for everyone and very much possible, but the only two things that I needed were faith and strength. And, I made it through. The irony in all of this is because I am actually 100% happy within, people think I am crazy. They believe I am delusional because I do not have any cares in the world. People actually think I am not processing life because I do not worry about anything, because I do not stress, because I am not sad and grossly mopey all the damn time, and because I can genuinely say I am happy and trying to get others to be happy, too. This, in itself, is the weirdest shit ever—something is completely wrong with me because nothing is wrong with me. All of these backward ass beliefs are part of the many reasons I wrote this book. I cannot believe people actually think this is okay and swear by the things that people are forced to believe by some of these quacks and others in society. It's more astonishing that "brilliant" clinicians, who take an oath to be tasked with objectively caring for humanity, also agree with putting someone's life in danger for absolutely no reason whatsoever other than their own personal gain. These people are using experimentation and theory, not reality in its truest form, to diagnose and treat people who are all suffering differently by using the same theoretical methods for each different person.

There is no one-size-fits-all method to mental health treatment and they can't always effectively cure emotions in a lab or from experimentation on others. The only thing these people should be doing is listening intently to their clients/patients so they can help them get rid of their emotional issues and mood problems, not drugging them to help them, ultimately, ignore the concerns. Science in itself was developed to generally help people understand how the Universe and everything in it works but with an inherent goal to be able to disprove God's existence. How can these people believe that constantly trying to experiment to dream up a cure in a test tube can fix or shut off something directly connected to God? And, I am the cuckoo. Cutting off our connection to God is why we have such a mentally unhealthy society. Like some loud celebrities and politicians out here, these people are "Christians," too. Certainly, not all doctors are like this because these good ones actually give their patients techniques to change their mindsets and work through the locus of the issue, but there are a great many who only see themselves first in every patient they see...or rather, their insurance companies since they will only be paid and remain employed if they can make it seem as if these mental health problems are incurable or drastic enough to require medical intervention. I give many kudos to those innovative doctors and therapists who understand that some mental chemical imbalances can be fixed in natural ways, like with mental exercises, soothing sounds and a calming CBD, or any natural, product as opposed to anti-anxiety meds that zombify them; and, are actually focused on doing what's best for the patient, not their money market accounts.

Mental health pertaining to emotions is not science in the respect that the person should be treated like a lab experiment. Emotions aren't rare anomalies, nor do they come about for unknown reasons. The context is different for every single person, but the foundation is *always* the same. I would think it's inhumane and unforgiving to observe people every day turning into the sickly walking dead not "living" amongst us just for these clinicians to be able to afford their mistresses' and wives' new fur coats and possibly supporting their own drug habits. Not every mental health professional is looking out for *your* well-being, despite the pieces of paper beautifully nailed to their walls saying they took an oath to actually give a shit. Psychology in itself is theoretical and experimental, and you must find what works for *you*, not the first thing someone else tells you or prescribes you. Have you ever wondered why there is no magic pill to erase all of our feelings and woes? Because we need to experience our feelings and also work through them for our journey—not get ridiculously high so we can keep sweeping the problem or trauma under an Afghan for someone to pull back one day and expose us all to consumption. Clean that shit up like you're supposed to!

I did not allow someone to experiment with my mood maladies because those nailed papers gave them a legal right to. After months of going through various escalating doses of one med; that med exacerbating or creating another issue that I had to take new meds for; the new meds having to be increased or paired with additional meds...I said fuck it and stopped all of it, detoxed, and turned inward. Simultaneously, the psych theories are someone else's dream and not necessarily a fix for me or others. Using people as lab rats to help them cope with different forms of melancholy is insanity in itself; and, the reason why people are these walking zombies believing they will never be okay again is they have the wrong people treating them. There are many of these "doctors" who will rail against any natural treatments, such as medical marijuana as a mental health treatment, and denigrate people who don't believe in their experimental or scientific theoretical beliefs, including colleagues in the same profession. You can Google how cutthroat scientists can be to other psychiatrists and scientists who think outside of the box. They are simply ignorant by definition, focusing on out of date non-facts or are truly not interested in curing you—only to keep you coming to them for the residual income your inner, unbalanced problems provide their bank accounts.

If mental health was about helping people, why is it almost unattainable because of the high rates being charged and hardly any insurance company covering it without the complaint being of a functional or life or death nature? You almost have to be standing naked in the middle of a busy highway before you will be taken seriously enough to get an insurance company to cover it. Otherwise, you have to choose between affording therapy sessions and feeding yourself and your family for a week, which is another social problem. That is why many low-income people can't get the treatment they need before it turns into substance abuse in trying to escape their pain, causing the stigma that low-income people are drug addicts and drunks, when they simply can't afford the treatment before it gets to this point. The same old domino effect plagues urban areas and the people of color in these areas because we have to factor in that Black people already have a different view of mental health treatment, to begin with, that runs from generations prior.

All in all, we must find our own innate courage and not totally entrust that, and any other part of our healing process, to people who lack their own courage and positive outcome experiences or are paid to minimize our courage so one "needs" to keep seeing them. However, we cannot find our courage or know any better if we're drugged out of our minds with the wrong shit. We put more trust in those "magic" pills and the people pushing them than we do in God or the people She actually ordained through becoming champions of their own path's trials, as Jesus did, to lead us back to our higher selves. It is quite alright to seek help to find the starting point of our healing because it can be difficult to do. We still have to take accountability for making it *through* the process, however.

Stopping midway is not an option for succeeding in our healing, nor is it the end of the journey just because one started on it. That's the mindset of overweight people that need to exercise to improve their health who work out one or two days their first week, then wonder why they haven't lost fifty pounds in that time and are ready to give up because working out is too hard. The work is continual and must be done until success happens in reaching complete happiness, and we do not stop once achieved; it just becomes easier. We must never stop fighting for what is truly ours—eternal happiness on earth.

Our brains are muscles and are just as important as our bodies and inner energies are to consistently exercise, keep healthy, passionately strengthen and protect. In antiquity, people didn't go to doctors when they had emotional or mood problems; they sought the help of high priestesses/priests and oracles to help them find their ways back to God and godly happiness since bad/unbalanced emotional and mood health, even if it is sparked by unresolved trauma, stems from spiritual disconnection (google the importance of spirituality in mental health and deeply research this to start your process if you suffer from mental health disturbances related to emotional and mood imbalances; immediately seek help if you ever feel suicidal because your life is always a gift that you should want). It is a concept that doctors shy away from because, among lots of things, it can come perilously close to rendering the profession, or its approaches in some areas, misguided. Jesus went through this same skepticism when he was simply telling people that God is in control but we control our happiness through our God-given free will—

particularly, if we follow God's Logos while here on earth. People called Jesus batshit and everything else negative because it was hard for people to believe that something they could not see controlled the forces in and around their lives. I am not sure of the pivotal chronological point when total faith in God changed to total faith in big pharma. However, I will bet heavy that it was when apothecaries started creating their own drugs centuries ago when things like coca plants, marijuana, and opium started becoming heavily regulated for the global governments' omnipresent control establishment or protecting some barons' profit, and they found lots of business in it being these few regulated channels with permission to distribute these special plants that expand consciousness. Sure, everyone likes to have a bump every now and then. That is a fun part of living, having a little excitement. But, happy zombies don't exist. They're too numb to feeling anything—psychedelic or bad.

The bottom line is, our faith and its trajectory are skewed, so we run to pharmacies or corner boys to fix something internal or that we broke in the first place. Who tears down their own house and cries because they're homeless, then loses faith because the cardboard replacement house they created isn't weatherproof? No matter what they build, it'll be a disaster because they won't have a solid foundation of structural integrity or impregnable protection that only boundless faith in God/Self provides. We have to put in the work. We have to be stronger than our weaknesses for our own sakes. We are a weak humanity, and I've truly never seen so much normalized backward shit in my lifetimes. Help me understand this ridiculousness, Lord. Jesus, don't take the wheel, just show me the roadmap so I can get the hell out of here...I'll drive damn myself.

"All happiness depends on courage and work."
~ Honore de Balzac

Diving back into the main point, we must maintain an untainted mindset that is our own. I am not suggesting we stop listening to people who are here to help us stay on the right path because we are gifted with circumstances and people for that very purpose. I am saying that each person needs to learn *when* to listen to others while being completely, *"in* our own." Don't be a dumb ass to yourself, in a nutshell. Some people just like being dumb asses and now is not one of those times because it only affects your life for the most part. Choosing to do something against helping yourself just for the sake of it or to be the stubborn person you may have always been is choosing to be a dumb ass. I do understand there is a learning curve, and some people learn things differently. I totally get that. I am not talking about you. I am specifically aiming at the calculated dumb dicks who purposely live their lives doing dumb shit for stupid fun and making other people's and their own lives hell.

The law of attraction is a very real thing. It is a pattern that has to be crafted well in order to work. We just need to dive a little deeper into a collective conscious whole in order to grasp it. The books and movies out on this subject only scratch the surface as the full information is dense and highly esoteric. In my studies, I have found great vision and understanding through the Kabbalah with some Buddhist and Taoist constructs peppering the way. Everyone learns differently, but this way is what spoke to me the clearest. Learning that the whole principle of higher living is about reciprocity (duality) explains so much about life and attainment. We have to give in order to receive, but when we receive. We give pleasure to the giver that energizes the entire transaction and amplifies the outcome, and we receive pleasure in pleasing and being thankful, or giving thanks, to the giver who is now receiving. Both entities give and receive, creating a cycle that keeps abundantly giving. If any part of the reciprocal circle is broken, then that cycle is, too. We cannot always go through life taking. Taking depletes. Positive energy behind giving never depletes; only the negative energy behind taking does. Now, this is not to be confused with receiving. It is okay to *receive,* but it is never okay to *take.* When one is given something, the giver is extending a part of themselves, including their own energy. They are giving of themselves (their energy) to you. That, in itself, is a gift as the positive energy extends from the soul.

Gifts are meant to be accepted with gratitude, no matter how small or trivial or how modest we are trying to be. When we deny, or block, receiving the gift given with good intent, it not only negatively affects the giver, but it also blocks our abilities to receive in the future from them and others. This also applies in the negative sense: if someone attempts to give to you maliciously, you can block that malice so that it goes back to the giver and is not received at all. When we give, we create an energetic tether that ties us to each other's energy (giver and receiver). We open that pathway once the giver extends their hand. All of this in simpler terms is if a friend who is having financial hardships decides to give you a gift, don't try to do them any favors by not accepting the gift. They have decided to majorly sacrifice to give you the gift for their own personal reasons. Taking away the pleasure they will feel in giving to you does nothing to help them or you whatsoever. It is not always about the money, even to someone who may be struggling financially at that time. It is about the action of giving, or as we have all heard before, *it is the thought that counts.* Giving may be the only pleasure this person gets in a life already full of anxiety and stress. They took the effort, put the thoughts and time into going out of their way to give to you, so they don't need you to throw it back in their face or send them away as if their good intentions were wrong to begin with. It is their choice to give, and it is not your responsibility to dictate to them that giving was wrong or to take away their choice to do so. Your actions could cause them to never give again, to anyone; thereby, interrupting their flow of blessings from the Universe. Sometimes we have to embody full altruism even in receiving (not taking). This is a very tricky action and requires ethical/moral standards to enact. It is a very deep principle that requires completed internal work to master and fully understand. If you are not in a place to fully receive in order to give and vice versa, then the abundance factor will not manifest in any of your outcomes. I talk about this extensively in other areas of my work. The bottom line is... Don't be an ignorant dumb ass!

Our thoughts for others are just as important as our own mindsets for ourselves. They also set us apart from those who have low-vibrating habits and mindsets, and those who live their lives not being accountable for their actions. We have to maintain a static set of rules in our waking lives to attach to our spiritual aspect. We are supposed to be living fully in our higher selves, but instead, we choose to live our earthly ones—in the ego. As mentioned previously, the ego is our heavy, burden-ladened material formation along with our physical aspect. Our spiritual being is supposed to be our guiding lights, not influencers on social media. We have it all backwards now, which is backwards in itself. Why would we ever want to be stressed all of the time and living a miserable existence? We wake up every day unhappy, having to purposely do the same things we are unhappy with. We actively put things in place in our lives to conform to this very unhappiness instead of trying to lighten our loads. What the hell kind of stupid logic is that? Society is blatantly telling us it is okay to live miserably and make others miserable simultaneously, and to do all the things that require misery in order to do it. That is what we vehemently follow because we have given up our free will to think to undeserving forces just to not be free of these familiar leashes. Why do we choose to live this way? I don't know because I do not live this way. I have always gone against the grain in never allowing people to tell me what I can and cannot do. If you want to be free again, then be free. Don't prevaricate. Don't find reasons why you need to be miserable and on an antidepressant the rest of your life. Nothing is stopping you from being free but you. Have that sex change; marry that prostitute you are in love with because she is human and both of you deserve love; you're a big burly straight man but you want to be a ballet dancer, so be it. Do whatever it is you truly want to do as long as you are not hurting yourself or others. Albeit lofty to some, the purpose of being free is so that hurt is no longer a factor of living a free life. It is all about where one ultimately wants to go and be, and staying that course. Pure happiness and love on my journey to Nirvana through a positive mindset and reciprocal actions is my ultimate attainment goal. What is yours?

"Happiness always looks small while you hold it in your hands, but let it go, and you learn at once how big and precious it is."
~Maxim Gorky

The lives of celebs and influencers are fantasies that some of us wish we can live. We can have those lives in ways that are fun and healthy, but as they pertain to our individualism. We can create our own fantasy lives just like they do and live in, and we don't have to succumb to the spiritual traps of trying to be exactly like them. We can still live authentically, even in our fantasies. It's not about money or looks; it's about our own creativity, positive self-image, and self-worth. If you possess these things, you can be whatever you want and live whatever glamorous life you choose as long as you also give back (secret beauty tips do not count!). Trying to live someone else's life or type of life hinders a person on every level, especially because they are neglecting parts of their own journey. This is especially true if you think you can only live the life of someone else in order to be happy. This even pertains to those who are not living their own lives because of others, like their parents. We are born to live our own lives to the utmost authenticity. Otherwise, only one person would exist on this planet if it were meant for all of us to live the same life. Always remember, only you can stop you from living the life you deserve, desire, and that was preordained by Source.

People often ask how we can have free will to live the lives we choose yet follow a predestined path. We were put here to do a job, and that's what God needs each of us to do. Everything else is up to us and will determine where we end up. An example of this is a person who spent a great portion of their lives in poverty as their journey while still choosing to help others in their plight. One of the many "Thousand Points of Light" living a life like this was Ms. Bea Gaddy, whom I had the opportunity to briefly meet, shake hands with, and serve alongside when I volunteered on a snowy Thanksgiving day at Dunbar High School in 1997. Their lives were meant to help others and their social and spiritual elevation was their reward as they continued to help people in the face of their own life's difficulties. The Bea Gaddy Family Center is one of the many causes I still give my holidays and donate to throughout each year until this day. Learn about her and the many unsung heroes across the country helping others and join them. We can do our heavenly jobs while living earthly lives as long as we never lose faith or stop doing what we were doing all along. It's the same as the job you are contracted to do when you applied, and when you clock in everyday. You are expected to do this job and are paid for your labor. However, once you clock out, you can live whatever life you choose to live. The minute you stop doing your job is the minute you lose the income that allows you to live the personal life you choose to live. Albeit, we can still choose to do other things in our own time, we are exponentially blessed when we choose to sacrifice that personal time to help others. As long as you are doing what God needs you to do, She will always have your back. Once you stop or veer off the path She had set, Source will no longer reward you. It's that simple. Notice how easy life is when you are happy and following your path. It only gets hard when we decide to do our own thing. I also can't say this enough—we don't know what's best, only God does, and we have to forever and wholeheartedly trust that.

All of our habits, patterns, and thoughts form our lives and how we live it, or exist in it for those still lost in their ego. They also affect others' lives in a fantastic or detrimental way. We have to be accountable for our actions and thoughts in all circumstances. No one else is responsible for them. We cannot blame anyone outside of ourselves for our problems and ways of thinking. You cannot be a dumb ass and expect the rest of humanity to fix your fuck-ups, then be mad when humanity doesn't respond. We are in a place with lots of characters and circumstances, so we must learn to navigate these waters without external finger-pointing when things go awry. Life is truly what we make it. We weave our own webs, so we deserve what we catch.

Facing Trauma

"Life will bring you pain all by itself. Your responsibility is to create joy."
~Milton Erickson

As an emotionally intelligent thought leader, life coach, and psychotherapist, I often work with people who have had major traumas in their lives and they struggle with healing, or beginning to heal. Many times, these people are very aware that they have these traumas but circumnavigate the effects created over time from holding on to or not fully resolving that trauma, instead of the opposite. There are many ways of resolving past trauma, but the most common ways people attempt to is avoidance and via an abuse or addiction of some kind. The first thing is that people avoid facing the trauma head on to work through it and relinquish all that comes along with holding on to it. The second is that traumatized people look to replace the happiness and good memories stolen from them by that trauma. They may find it in the high they get from alcohol, drugs, or other vices that give them a sensation of living or *feeling* something (dangerous adrenaline-inducing behaviors, cutting, abusing others, etc.—a person's self-prescribed medication can come in many forms). I am not talking about dangerous psycho- or sociopaths who get off on cutting the tail off of live cats because they have severe mental disturbances. For the sake of keeping this book simple, I am *only* referring to people who have experienced trauma at some point in their past and never worked through it, and now suffer from and struggle with common mental health issues such as anxiety and depression. However, I have discovered that a good portion, not all, of the aforementioned -paths have underlying traumas that severely developed into something else. Some people's traumas have turned into the proverbial demons that prohibit the full enjoyment of one's life and have manifested into something that has taken its own form. This can be seen in the -paths, too. Some people are so scarred by past traumatic events that they begin to take on other ways of being or thinking in order to make living more tolerable. Sometimes, in dangerous ways.

For those of us who have experienced trauma that has affected our ways of navigating life and having meaningful interpersonal relationships, there is always still hope for complete happiness and a life of peace and promise. So many people believe that once they are diagnosed with a mental health problem, like being bipolar or having depression, life is completely over, which is lightyears far away from the truth. Facing trauma, also, does not mean reliving it; it means many other things like recognizing what its existence is doing to our current lives, forgiving the people who caused us the pain, returning the (energy of) blame or fault they forced on us (if applicable), and letting it go. Forgiving and letting go are the most critical parts of healing in any circumstance, and, also, the two most difficult ones. Anything outside of that on the good or bad side of the spectrum is our choice. As a very sensitive example, if a woman is raped and she now has problems with men, she has to be able to forgive her assailant, not allow his actions to take any more of her life away, and give back to him the trauma, or the energy of it, that he caused so that she can fully forgive him and let it all go. In that instance, she will reclaim and rebuild her power and strength. The rapist can no longer take her strength. The rapist, society, or even she, can no longer make her feel guilty about the incident. The rapist can no longer affect her relationships with men or keep her so scared that she never leaves the house. None of these feelings can happen again unless she allows it to happen. Fear and guilt from others shouldn't happen in the first place, of course, but these traumas set in in different ways for different people and depend on the support systems in place for the victim at the time of the incident and thereafter. No one can take anything from us unless we give it away, especially after traumatic situations.

I have had people look at me sideways when I say that forgiveness is the way. Their verbal response is usually, "I'm not forgiving shit. He can die as far as I am concerned." However, holding on to the anger and wanting revenge keeps the trauma heavy on us and unable to heal. I'd rather heal than be stuck with having nightmares every night replaying the whole ordeal or lugging around the heaviness of the hate, never experiencing complete happiness. Society, also, has to stop contributing to the madness in blaming people on the receiving end for these types of traumatic events as it makes it harder for these people to survive them. This is not helpful at all. Giving perpetrators excuses is the same as condoning their actions. We need to give the victims—male or female—compassion and support. Making the women in these situations the pariah in their own trauma is a particular problem that women face far too often but *all* of us have a responsibility to come together to channel our feminine energy to help them bolster their strength and regain their power.

121

Not to veer off of the point of trauma that all of us as people face, but this is yet another example of a disgusting symptom of the unfeeling patriarchal, or predominantly masculine energetic, world we live in. We need to enforce compassion, not making the victims feel like it is their fault it happened to them.

"Anyone can hide. Facing up to things, working through them, that's what makes you strong."
~Sarah Dessen

This is why it is always important we maintain our own strength and sense of self so that no matter what happens on our journeys, no one can ever take any of it away from us—no matter what. I will continually reiterate that no one can take anything from us unless we *allow* it to be stolen or freely *give* it away. I know some folks will say it is easier said than done in a lot of cases depending on the severity of the trauma, but it still boils down to resilience, strength, our faith in ourselves, and the Higher Power. God will never give us anything we cannot bear, and we are fully equipped to handle what it is that we need to bear for our journeys. So, the idea that something is easier said than done comes from a place where people are either hesitant to face the trauma for fear of reliving it or afraid to face the trauma for the existence of the fear itself. It can be easy if we stop resisting doing the work and letting fear hamper any healing progress. If we went through the trauma and are alive to discuss it, we can get through facing it to put it in its place. We impose fears and other irrelevant things on ourselves. We create and add these layers to our problems, and that, in itself, is a problem. In other words, we often carve out the biggest crosses out of the heaviest wood we can find to carry on our paths before we have to hang ourselves upon them. We subsequently become hesitant to fix something so grievous that we stagnate ourselves. We choose to do nothing as opposed to fixing it and getting rid of it before it turns into something much worse. No matter how many times I have heard, "...but it is hard, you just don't understand," it always brings our conversation back to the person's faith and inner strength. Think about it in this example:

You break your leg in one place, but you're too afraid to go to the ER (bills, pain, whatever the fear) to get it fixed. Instead, you do nothing or simply put a bandage on it to heal any damaged flesh but not the bone. Your leg heals, but you now cannot walk on this leg; it is infected and it is more painful than it was when you broke it. The leg will either have to be amputated or saved, but saving it will require you to have it broken in several places for it to be reset, and the recovery time will be lengthy and more strenuous than previously...and more costly (much more missed time from work, rehab therapy, various medical equipment— such as braces, casts, etc., follow-up visits possibly not covered by insurance, transportation to get to these places because you cannot drive...the list goes on). All you had to do in the first place was tend to it then.

Holding on to things, or attachment, never ends well. We are made of light and not meant to be attached to the heavy energy of traumatic encounters with people or events—only happy memories that are light. We tend to hold on to trauma and the negative emotions from them for various reasons (comfort, learned negative behavior, as a bad, unhelpful way of protection, the grief of a lost loved one keeps them front of mind, etc.). This does not mean that the rape victim cannot carry mace to protect herself or learn martial arts for self-defense. It means she cannot go through life as an agoraphobic, afraid of ever encountering unknown men, or assuming every man she crosses paths with will rape her. I do understand that not everyone is strong out of the gate after traumas, but I do not believe that giving excuses for people who have been traumatized and *refusing* to recover, when there are many ways available (some are free!) to heal, is conducive to their necessary recovery. Coddling those who have been through trauma longer than the initial comfort and subsequent support on the road to recovery gives them the green light to prolong beginning their recovery process, find ways around the recovery process, or not recover at all. I am not trying to be harsh, but this is really what some people do. They expect people to be sympathetic to them not ever leaving the house because of being fearful of people thirty years after the incident or not understanding why others who have lost a loved one aren't mopey like they are about theirs and feeding into their inability or refusal to see grief differently than as a sad way to live the rest of one's life. At this point, it is their responsibility to take charge, and no one should feel obligated to cater to this person's requirements or whims. There are no rules or specific timeframes on how or when a person should fully recover—the same as grief—but there is one on healthily *starting* the recovery process itself. You, sometimes, cannot start a healthy healing process if your support system or internal strength is lacking at onset, but you, also, cannot be and remain strong if you do not have unwavering internal strength and/or a good support system throughout the ups and downs of recovery, and in keeping the residual issues away indefinitely. Strength is the constant factor on one's path.

There are so many damaged people in the world, mostly by the hands of others, and people have been conditioned to believe that those who are actually okay within themselves are unbalanced as opposed to the ones with actual mental diagnoses. How often do we see a person skipping down a hallway or street and we give them a look like what the fuck is wrong with them or make fun of their happiness? Is it so unusual to see a person happy about their lives or even just being happy in that moment? Classic deflection, fighting accountability, or, quite simply, wanting others to be miserable is entirely what this is. People have to realize that hurt people who are struggling with trauma end up hurting more people, particularly the ones who love them the most. This creates more hurt people and more people unnecessarily fighting other people's battles. This is another perfect example of our actions and decisions affecting others' lives.

"Success is not final, failure is not fatal: it is the courage to continue that counts."
~Winston S. Churchill

Human nature is to run into a corner and lick our wounds when we are hurt. Animals do this, but they do not stay in this position longer than necessary because they, then, are seen as weak prey to predators. Even a weak or wounded lion can be killed by a stronger lion or even a hyena if that lion stays in a weak position. They lie low, lick their wounds, then keep it moving once healing has begun; they do not stay low. Some humans do not fully emerge from their trauma. There is nothing on this earth that is traumatizing enough to not allow oneself to heal or emerge as a newly formed butterfly. These events are lessons and for our own growth on our paths. We should never stay knocked down. We were born resilient. The human body has its own healing mechanisms but it is our job for us to heal our Souls. When we don't fully experience the situation from onset to healing, we slight ourselves the full human experience as meant by those events and lessons. So, we sometimes end up having to learn them all over again by going through the same lessons multiple times. We also do not fully blossom into the beautiful flowers God needs in her Garden to help others in humanity see the pulchritude in life. Just like the body needs to heal when it's injured, our energies and minds need the same attention. We tend to separate mind from body, but it's all part of the same trinity that includes our Souls. Body and Soul cannot be treated as separate singular afterthoughts. They need to be tended to like any garden of growth, together, while on this plane of existence. Our bodies are the temples for our Souls, which is our connection to God as Her children in Her Garden. Trauma is a fertilizer that can also kill our gardens if it is not properly utilized only for the bugs.

Grief during bereavement is an area of trauma that is a little different. Loss of a loved one is very traumatic for a lot of people, especially if the loss is a parent/guardian, friend, spouse, or just someone who had a very large portion of our hearts. Healing is a lot harder to do because we want to have all of that person with us—not just memories, there is nothing we can do to bring them back, and we don't want to let go for the best interest of both parties. I had to watch my aunt—the one who raised me during my younger years—slowly die of lung cancer over a four month period while her own children didn't give a shit until she ended up on her deathbed. Everyday I watched her keep this secret while she went from being a healthy-sized woman with bird legs and a beer belly (we joked about this) to being less than a hundred pounds. I would hear her, literally, cough up her lungs then, when checking in on her, I would see blood everywhere as she tried to hide it. I remember begging her to tell everyone what's going on or to let me take her to get treatments and I would keep it secret if she wanted me to, but she just did not want to be a burden, no matter how much I cried and told her she could never be a burden to any of us or how I phrased how her loss would tear us apart. After I saw how happy she was in the hospital room, I realized she was just tired and looking forward to her final rest. No matter how much I wanted her to stay on this planet, surrounded by selfish, shitty people, I had to let her go. As many funerals I have gone to since I was a kid, hers was the only one I attempted to jump in the grave as they lowered her casket. My uncle and cousin had to pull me up because I refused to let go of the only love I knew. That one was a hard loss to get through almost twenty years ago...until this year topped them all.

We will never be prepared for losing a parent. We struggle with acknowledging our loved one has departed. We don't want to admit to ourselves that we will never see them again. We don't want to forget them so we create rituals, like celebrating their birthdays or saving a place for them at the holiday table. But, do we ever get over the idea of not seeing them again? Is not seeing them the reason why some of us can't seem to recover from the loss? Are we being selfish to want them to be here with us in a place that we can't even get along with one another and blaming our Creator when it is God's Will they are gone? If we had a better understanding of death, we would not bereave as much as most of us do when we lose a loved one. We would understand that we all have the capability to connect with them in our dreams and prayers, and even in our waking lives, for those of us knowledgeable or gifted in this way, until we arrive where they are. They are not gone and never far away from us. Just call on them and they will be there, just like God.

Of all of the deceased people who visited me, there was never any heartache or pain. They were always happy and having that ethereal glow—their light shining bright. They were no longer encumbered by ailments, bills, pain, or living in a world where everyone hates and hurts everyone. Why would I selfishly want my loved one living here when they are happy—sometimes, the happiest they've ever been—just so I can be satisfied? I do not like being sad or depressed, so I found a way to honor my mom as opposed to being selfish in wanting her here or uselessly mad that she is not. I also did not do an ostentatious funeral or memorial because they are only for the living and for people who suck at being there more often in people's lives. Besides the fact that she didn't want any of that but left the decision up to me, she only wanted her body donated to science, which I respectfully did. It didn't kill me and it's not killing me to do it this way as part of my healing process. In fact, it makes me happier because I know that she is proud of me and what I am doing for others. It does not mean I don't miss her with everything in me and I don't have my moments. Of course I do, and my aunt, too. I have decided to be happy for them not suffering anymore and believe that they are truly in a better place than here—a place where all of our loved ones are finally at peace. We will never dishonor or forget them in this thought process because their love and memories of being a part of our lives will never go away. We just recognize that grief is not what they would want for us, and that happiness is what we unselfishly want for them. Being sad and grieving is not the only way we know and show them that they are greatly missed. They already know it. However, can they really rest in peace if they see we are hurting and not living, since they no longer have the opportunity, or are we being selfish again—to ourselves and them?

Why do we proactively choose and prefer to stay painfully broken, continually doing the things that pulverize the remaining crumbles of our former selves before the trauma, instead of doing the internal work to permanently heal? Have we been programmed to believe that healing is impossible? If the latter is true, why do we so easily accept that as reality; and, why do we seek help to heal, doing things that we know won't help (e.g. seeing doctors & therapists for years, taking a ton of psychotropic meds, not doing anything differently ourselves & obviously making no progress in the healing process, yet still suffering from mental health disturbances), all while knowing we won't follow through to its success?

"It's not the load that breaks you down, it's the way you carry it."
~Lou Holtz

Fear

"Nothing in life is to be feared, it is only to be understood. Now is the time to understand more, so that we may fear less."
~Marie Curie

Fear is another area where many people struggle. Fear is also another creation of the ego. People are terrified to face their pasts or know the possibilities of their futures. We were born fearless. As we know, or should know by now in our evolution journey, fear is nothing but *false evidence appearing real*. Why would we ever want to live our lives based on something that isn't really there? Well, many people do...a lot of people do. We see it every day with racism, people with addictions, and those who have unchecked trauma that has taken an unprecedented form in their lives. These are just a few ways fear can take over one's life and affect others' lives in an impactful way. There are ways to combat fear, but the methods are deeply rooted in faith in oneself, resilience, and overall strength. In my work, I have discovered that resilience and strength are one and the same. Although they are two different words, you cannot have one without the other. We are not born with fears, but we develop them over time. An example would be telling a child not to jump on the bed because they could fall and bump their head on the corner of a nightstand or otherwise injure themselves. When the child does not listen and finally falls, they learn their lesson by the pain they endure from the fateful injury. They will either continue to jump on the bed but with finesse or be completely stunted by the fear of injuring themselves again. In this example, we can see how fear can change the perspective of a person scarred by a traumatic event and how they move forward after that trauma. They have the strength to not allow the fear to stop them from finding safer ways of doing something; learning that this thing they are doing is, in fact, unsafe; or, they will never be able to do this thing, or even similar things, again for fear of being injured, or worse. Being scared is not a substitute for being safe. Fear is also, sometimes, one of the many masks of grief.

"Don't be afraid of your fears. They're not there to scare you. They're there to let you know that something is worth it."
~C. JoyBell C.

Fear is an indication of where we are spiritually. Because our higher selves are divine, the closer we are to that divinity and divinely guided, the more freely we can live without fear of something detrimental coming our way. We are also one with the premise that when it is our time to go, it will not matter how cautious we are. Once we rise to higher levels of vibration, we will lose all aspects of the ego and gain more traits of the divine. People who are spiritually closer to the divine do not possess fear, and they are exponentially happier. When we are laden with anxieties and fears, we have no room for anything positive to infiltrate and replace the lower vibrating energies. Heavier items are harder to move; thereby, making it more difficult to make room for lighter things. What would be better and easier to carry...a glass full of water or a glass full of rocks? The container and volume are the same, but the contents we put in to determine the weight depends on us. If we are afraid to properly fill the container with the right things, we affect our ability to go through life with the least weight and the most ease. We cannot let fear from one experience ruin future experiences or any part of our natural way of existence. Fears from experiences can spill over into other parts of our lives—like, into our relationships. Yet, another instance where our actions or unnecessarily created situations affect others. Like the egos that says we are and know better than God, fear should not exist. And, for those just needing a little boost of courage in a few words...grow a pair!

"Fear kills everything. Your mind, your heart, your imagination."
~ Cornelia Funke

Addictions & Substance Abuse

This is a very complex subject and there are stigmas associated with seeking therapy in general, let alone for the addiction or substance abuse problem itself. Additionally, people who suffer from substance abuse are sometimes embarrassed that they have this ailment to contend with, making them more apprehensive to seeking help. People who have an addiction or abuse a substance are addicted to the feeling they feel from engaging with the object of the addiction and not the drug itself. The feeling substances like heroin provide is the euphoric feeling of being hugged by God or, for the atheist, like being hugged by clouds while straddling a unicorn pooping rainbows. It is purely ineffable. People who struggle with an addiction almost always have a trauma they are hiding or running from or are missing the happiness that naturally helps us produce the same euphoric feelings. Even in some supposed hereditary mental health situations, such as depression, there are holistic ways to rid individuals of their ailments with extensive internal work and psychotherapy, not more drugs that alter or trick the mind. I do understand that prescription psychotropic medications help those who need instantaneous results but finding a healthier solution to help them to permanently eliminate the issue should be a part of their treatment, too. For example, I have seen numerous people get a handle on their occasional anxiety and depression, and eventually eradicate it, by using St. John's Wort; sometimes, alongside psychotherapy. However, pharmaceutical companies can't make billions on the mental health market if everyone is taking something that naturally grows on Gaia to aid in their emotional healing. Simultaneously, healthy use of natural herbs or unnatural drugs that help us 'see' spiritually can be of use in mental health treatment. I am not telling people to do these drugs on their own but I am telling people to do their own research for what works or may work for them.

Moving back into the point, more drugs do nothing but keep substance abusers in the mindset that they will never be okay and will always need the help of some kind of drug to help or make them function "normally." The proof is in the fact that it is very possible to beat, and plenty of people have managed to beat addictions, substance abuse and their lifelong (or short-term) traumas. Individuals are out here seeking help, but the sciences will put people further back into their progress by changing the form in which they deal with the abuse and life, as opposed to helping them identify and indefinitely eradicate the underlying issue that causes the need for an agonist. An example of this that I have seen is individuals on drugs meant to help them with narcotic addictions or dependence but, in fact, still keeps them addicted to the drugs; it only helps them to not overdose. Although it may help them chemically, it does not take away the cravings for the euphoric feeling if, for some of them, there is a mental health concern being swept under a rug. This made me think that there is a deeper sociological conspiracy going on that I will not go into. However, these "rehab" drugs seem to be just legalized (and lucrative) versions of the same drugs the clients struggle with just possessing an added safeguard to prevent overdose. I know it acts duly to eliminate or minimize cravings and quell withdrawal symptoms in recovering addicts, but this is not alcohol where it is believed that having the hair of the dog will relieve a hangover.

The approach cannot be the same in all cases of alcohol and drug abuse. It is very hard to overcome these addictions or dependence, especially now when people are trying to escape what the world has become. There are many arguments on the effectiveness of a modified opiate to help with recovery, but these drugs *do* help some people. However, there needs to be more attention paid to the underlying problem with each individual at their psychosocial entryway. Once new methods are widely employed, doctors and therapists can concurrently and safely reduce then eliminate the cravings and help with the transition back to owning one's own life. The single positive of these drugs is that it is almost impossible to overdose on, unless combined with other drugs that suppress breathing, for example. Otherwise, I have seen repeatedly where these drugs just keep people in the same position they were in of wanting an ever upgrading high. They either relapse or die trying to find a better high. I have witnessed very few people conquer their problem on these drugs. They still feel the need to get high because they can never get high enough on these drugs. Not all addicts, just some. We see this a lot with celebrities who either suffer in silence then we hear of their overdoses or suicides, or those who are in and out of rehab until rehab can't help them anymore and they end up like the others. They needed our help, love and support and, somewhere and somehow, we failed them. My heart was shattered when I heard about Chester Bennington a week before my birthday a few years back. Reanimation and Meteora were the soundtracks to my early through mid 20s. He overcame his drug and alcohol issues at one point but he slipped because he still struggled with depression. You could tell in his lyrics as they spoke so loudly, which I could, also, relate to as I struggled with issues during this time. He is an example of why we absolutely need to include nuanced mental health treatment in substance abuse treatment.

We must remember that most addictions are usually a symptom of a deeper or larger problem, and those problems are the catalyst for the addiction. To help all of our brothers and sisters who struggle with addiction, we must first stop judging them for having it, then help them through it. We do not know their journey or what trauma(s) they endured in life that makes living unbearable. Most of us have had unbearable life moments but they affect us all differently. If someone loses a loved one and decides to start drinking, we cannot make them feel "less than" because they are struggling with their grief. They do not need our judgments; they need our help, love, and support, alongside grief counseling, and to remind them of their own inner strength over their addiction and grief. Many suffer in silence because of widespread judgment and become one of the many numbers in statistics of overdoses and suicides. Once they realize they have positive support, they can seek the help they need without the burden of someone else's poor, selfish (mis)judgment that is likely based on their own personal prejudices from their own trial-filled journey. I am sure they would want the same compassion, consideration and understanding if this was their situation. The clear bottom line is that these people do not need to be judged but helped, and the help needs to be in the form of finding and addressing the locus that sparked the addiction, not giving them more reasons to be addicted or more drugs to be addicted to. Just think back to antiquity when people were only addicted to pleasing God. If only we can return back to that, our highs would be constant and natural, like that rainbow-pooping unicorn I mentioned earlier. Faith and happiness were their drugs of choice.

"Even if you're on the right track, you'll get run over if you just sit there."
~Will Rogers

Feeling and Thought Mediocrity

"Joy came always after pain."
~Guillaume Apollinaire

As humans, we are built with these things called emotions or feelings. When faced with adversity, we tend to wallow in those feelings of disappointment instead of understanding that everything does truly happen for a reason, and to trust the Universe's process. I always hear people justify shutting down after getting bad news of a situation not going their way or focusing on the disappointment of the adverse situation itself. There is nothing that should be able to take our happiness or positivity away at any point in life. People have given too much credence to negative emotions. Negative emotions chip away at any happiness we possess, automatically lowers our vibrations and causes us unnecessary mental distress. It is extremely hard to get to a one hundred percent happy level, so why would we allow a situation that won't matter in minutes, hours, or even a couple of days ruin what we strive for over a lifetime? It just makes no sense. It is okay to stop and reflect on a situation to fully understand what happened, sure, but not to let it overwhelm one's life in the moment to where they are snapping at random people or the ones they love, or taking those frustrations out on people, especially any children in that person's life. Everything can be resolved, so there is no reason why people should be mentally, verbally, or sometimes physically abused by people who cannot handle what life occasionally throws their way. This is never okay and opens the door for continual issues and circumstances that are set up to disappoint. We have already discussed that it is never okay to mistreat someone, so it begs to say that it is never okay to mistreat yourself.

Our thoughts steer our actions. Once we have made a habit of always having positive thoughts, it will be easier to handle adverse situations and life itself will become much easier to bear and more enjoyable and pleasant. If we have low-level thoughts, we will have low-level actions resulting in low-level outcomes. If you believe you are a failure, you will fail at everything you believe you will fail at. There is a stark contrast between believing and knowing. Beliefs can be altered or changed. Knowing, or having knowledge, is pure power and cannot be altered or taken from us—only expounded or improved upon. We must have ironclad positive thoughts, or negative knowledge will turn against us. They cannot be flimsy, fear-based, or negative, even in a fleeting manner. Every single thought must be of integrity, positivity and truth. Wishing something harmful on another person in order to obtain something great does not count toward our own positive thoughts and will result in a negative outcome for the wisher. We must be steadfast and thorough in our commitment to being and doing better as individuals for the collective to evolve properly. Since our thoughts are also energy that travels distances, we need to make sure the tethered line we cast with those thoughts attached to the end of it is equally moral in nature. As mentioned in this book many times, what we throw out is what we get back, no matter the form it departed as. It is absolutely paramount that we do our part as individuals during this time in our human evolution, so we do not, again, set in motion the chain of events that led us to the perilous position we are currently in as this tainted version of the human race— essentially, undoing any collective spiritual progress.

It is wonderful that emotional intelligence is making a resurgence. I use the word "resurgence" because it is not new. In antiquity, people used others' emotions and thoughts in every single action of theirs to determine what they were to do. We are the exact opposite today—we only think of ourselves first and everyone else last. Emotional intelligence (and thought leadership) is being thrown around in the business world a lot now, also, which is great because the loss of its prominence in business processes started when greed for wealth developed. Humanity is being led back to its original state of Soul/Spirit first without material being a factor or the very first thought. We have to get back to putting other people's needs ahead of our own. I am not talking about forgetting the value of self-care. We cannot be any good to anyone else if we are not whole ourselves. After we have done the internal work, only then can we be wholehearted in our actions and be able to contribute to humanity.

Ignorance is not bliss. Being purposely ignorant does not protect one from the truth, especially ignorance of other individuals' emotions and their plights. It actually stunts our growth and filters knowledge of the maladies plaguing the surrounding world, the causes of them, and the people in the world suffering from these earthly troubles. One tends to ignore what is right in front of them. An example of this is when a person is aware they are doing bad things to people, but they use retaliatory excuses or willful blindness to their actions as their reasoning for not seeking help or, otherwise, fixing their issues.

This last point can settle comfortably into other sections of this book. However, I settled it here because it is apropos given that this issue invariably affects our inner growth and thoughts that ultimately determine our success at achieving a wealth of inner and outer happiness. Communication is a very difficult, nuanced thing, and proper execution is *the* critical factor in being able to fluidly move through a world full of different people and to be able to live in this world interpersonally. People, or should I say adults, don't properly communicate anymore. I have rarely seen a child hold their tongue. They usually say what is on their minds to ensure others know how it is that they feel. It is only as they are molded into the adults we want them to become that censorship becomes the way. Adults stop speaking to each other instead of fixing the problems between them. After communication has been had and the differences are found to be irreconcilable, only then should the two adults part ways. There remains a world of bad energy in the atmosphere from unresolved relationship tensions simply because people don't really talk anymore.

I have had people stop speaking to me because they don't like me but they don't really have a reason of their own as to why. Most of these were situations of miscommunication with the remainder being from judgment on their part. I have had people dislike me before we even met. For what, you ask? I haven't a clue. Maybe because it was a Monday; everybody hates Mondays, who knows! However, they're likely going off of other people's dislikes and prejudices instead of forming their own informed opinions of the type of person I am by meeting and getting to know me. That is how I met my wife. She hated me and had never met me. Once she met me and got to know who I was, it was a wrap. I had been going through life trying to figure out what happened between me and certain people, only to find out over time that they just flat out didn't like me for no reason, or one they were willing to admit. I have my suspicions on what the reasons may be. I have even had a person I befriended but did not really talk to very much who was in a fruitless marriage before I met them randomly contact me and blame me for their divorce after their new partner broke up with them five years later. FIVE YEARS! This person always had self-esteem issues and needed someone to blame because of the usual "no one wanting to be with me" mentality and not wanting to be alone, so they would take the first person to give them attention or take their frustrations out on any person they could. Every time she broke up with someone after her divorce, she would do this. So, after I got tired of being contacted only to be talked to this way, I finally politely told her, in a nutshell, to go back to her ex-husband if he'll have her and be the miserable bitch that she still seemed to be so I can stop being blamed for her lifelong misery. The problem is she was an unhappy person, to begin with, and was looking for others to give her happiness, instead of her finding it within herself first, as I have always told her. The reasons usually are really that childish, full of insecurity or, simply, miscommunication.

Some also think I'm stuck up or a bitch. That's cute. And, one ex-friend foolishly assumed because he turned 55, I grew into not wanting to be around him solely because of his age when, in fact, age was one of the paramount reasons he mattered to me in the first place the 25 years we were good friends. Obviously, for 25 years, he was always older than me, so this is clearly a blatant insecurity of his own that I was accused of creating when I gave him no such inclination of anything near what he believed. Never once in 25 years. I only found out because I had to ask him why he just disappeared in the middle of our regular conversation, and I was contacting him as normal with no responses. I asked him when did I say this or where did it come from. I have died thrice already because I am still holding my breath waiting on his— what better be—passionate reason to cause him to randomly cut off a wonderful friendship after 25 years with no clear evidence of his claims. These are all laughable, insecure reasons to end friendships, especially long ones, but if that's what they want, so be it. I will still get my 80 winks. They just made it extremely clear they no longer belong in my life and on my journey, and made it so much easier for their exit—they found the door without me having to show it to them. It is so not a loss for me. For those who I have had an encounter with (as opposed to the random delusions of the people above), there is still usually an immature reason because I haven't done anything to anyone like burned down their home, grand theft or attempted to kill them, so anything outside of these things is fixable—and, even one or two of these can be salvageable in some ways. Sure, when I was younger, I had confrontations and such but that's what young people do. Most of it was he-say-she-say or just disagreements over stupid shit. I am not sure any of this Karma still exists for me because part of my over-a-decades-long journey of finding myself and learning was to reach out to these people and make amends. However, if they are still holding feelings, isn't it about time for them to get over it? I'm good.

Even Andre Risen forgave Lisa "Left Eye" Lopes for burning down his home, and he still loved her because he saw how angelic she was inside. God rest her beautiful soul. In these encounters of mine, I feel like for it to be this easy for these people to feel the way that they do or did, some resentment had to have been there to begin with. Who knows why these things happen because these adults don't communicate properly, but they are heard loud and clear when they have something negative to say about me or to chime in when someone else does. It's ridiculous that "adults" act the way children should be acting. I sincerely hope they find peace within themselves so they don't feel like they need to strongly dislike me, hate me, or be angry with what they don't like about themselves where deflection gives them their five low-vibrating minutes of pleasure. My door has always been open for people to present the issues they have with me, but nobody ever does. They just walk away mad and angry, carrying that load with them. How can we resolve issues or amicably part ways if we don't communicate about the issues? Some people just enjoy their misery because it's what they're used to. Others don't want other people's lights to shine and deliberately attempt to dim them because they're afraid to or won't allow their own light to burn bright. It's usually as simple as those things. Judgment, fear, and poor perspectives of life are their enemies, not me or anyone else. Some of these same people in my personal experiences are alcoholics, substance abusers, or gluttons for punishment...but I'm the problem. The irony is since I've separated from these people over the years, I've grown exponentially, but they're still unhappy people stuck in the same low-vibrating thoughts and ways. Yet, again, even in my absence, I'm the problem, though, if you ask them. Why?

This isn't just the people in my experiences. I'm sure I'm not the only person who experienced purely cynical or miserable people in their lives, always trying to piss on other people's parades because theirs had a low-quality turnout. Always

144

remember, if a person judges you before they actually know you or generally dislikes you when you did absolutely nothing to them, the problem is not you—it is within them. Please don't take on their demons no matter how much they try to convince you it is you who made them act or feel that way. You cannot make them feel this way; they are choosing to feel this way. If years have gone by and your name is still on their lips, be proud of how important you must be to them because you are clearly an aspiration that they'll never reach. You're a goal to them. They cannot even be their authentic selves without drowning it in alcohol, drugs, judgment, anger, deflection, hate, and so on, so they definitely won't reach you or your vibrational heights if they employ these actions or emotions. Don't gloat or be proud because that can backfire on you. Also, don't lower your vibrations by stooping to their level in being mad at them and/or the situation. Be happy because you must be doing something right and move on from them. I'd say you have mastered this part of communication if they're getting your picture without your words.

All in all, I always say just "be" to people. For my life, I have assigned the acronym the words, "beyond existence." The sole meaning—being limitless. We are just existing right now, and we are not being who we are supposed to. We exist in someone else's box. We are *being* executives, *being* students, *being* parents, *being* what society wants us to *be*. None of us are just *being*...freely. I'm not saying we aren't these amazing things, but these things should not define our soul's purpose or who we are, unless it is our specific journey. When we put words behind *be*, we are putting limitations on our existence. That is another way we stifle our evolution. *Beyond existence* is precisely what it means. Beyond just existing just to exist, especially in those positions. *Bey*ond mundanity. *Bey*ond existence, there is vast limitlessness. It is like looking out over the sea of your soul and not seeing any land in sight. From your shores, you can sail anywhere.

Golden Rule

"Love is that condition in which the happiness of another person is essential to your own."
~Robert Heinlein

It seems that we are lost on what this is. It seemingly went right out of the window as soon as it was written. Many people still do not know what it is. I am appalled that another human does not know what the Golden Rule is. How have they lived their lives to date if this is a foreign concept to them? How have they been treating people all of this time if this principle was unbeknownst to them? I shudder to think about the loads of people left destitute on their path. In any case, it strictly showcases what's wrong with this world. People do not actively put in the effort to care for one another before themselves or as themselves. Before the question arises in the mind, I have already said that it is okay for self-care; I am speaking generally about altruism at this point. I have watched people witness an accident with injuries, video it while passing, or not stop to help because they were late for work but use said accident as the reason they were late as if they actually intervened by providing aid. Not only is that a piss poor humanly thing to do, but they effectively capitalized on someone else's misery. Meanwhile, these same people wonder why they have stacks of problems.

Supporting certain causes doesn't represent your exact support of the cause per se; it has everything to do with supporting another human being's happiness and freedoms. Supporting others' right to be free and happy shouldn't be hypocritical; it should be something you do simply as being a good damn human being. You don't have to agree with the cause—LGBT+ causes for example, but you need to agree that everyone deserves happiness and love no matter what form it takes. One's decision to love someone of the same sex may not be agreeable to you but fighting or voting against an inane piece of legislature (which shouldn't even be a thing) that says they cannot marry who they choose is essentially agreeing that they do not deserve happiness and love because *you* believe God said they don't or *you* believe God won't love them anymore as it is an abomination. So, now it's up to *you* to determine someone else's happiness? So, it is up to *you* to decide for God what Her children do with their own heart and lives? So, the entire LGBT+ community has to suffer because *you* think *you* know better? Okay. So, how happily married are *you*? How happy are *you* in general? If you cannot say you are a million percent happy and have unconditional, unwavering love from a significant other or spouse, sit your miserable ass down and let someone else be what *you* are not. The right for someone to love another is a God-given right, not a church, state, miserable society's or other type of fabricated privilege. You have no say-so over that whatsoever, and you cannot in good "Christian" conscience say that you are about equality or inclusion yet pick and choose who deserves it. So, I guess you are one who believes women shouldn't have total control over their bodies, Black people should not be treated as human beings and people should be locked in cages and starved to death because they just want the same freedoms as other human beings on this planet. Yeah, all of that sounds good and precisely what God wants you to do. God does not pick and choose who She loves or gives rights to. She also did not directly give anyone walking this planet the authority for any of these decisions. No one! This includes the papacy. If this world were reverse, you would not find it fair to have to fight to be able to love and marry your hetero partner as God promised love to everyone She created. You would feel you deserve that right to love that person, too. Also, saying you don't care what people do behind closed doors but you just don't want it in your face does not excuse you from this idiocy. Unless you live with an LGBT+ person, what they do behind their closed bedroom door is still none of your business. And, if it bothers you so much, move the fuck out and deal with this personal issue of your own behind your own closed door. Do not advocate for laws saying that LGBT+ people bother you. It has nothing to do with you. It has everything to do with there not being judgment or restrictions on someone else's free will to love because of your own internal and religious insecurities or misunderstandings. Shouldn't everyone be entitled to love, or are we that selfish that we advocate against it because we do not want everyone to know it since we lack it unconditionally for ourselves?

"Thou shalt love the Lord thy God with all thy heart, and with all thy soul, and with all thy mind. This is the first and greatest commandment. And the second is like unto it. Thou shalt love thy neighbor as thyself. On these two commandments hang all the law and the prophets."
Matthew 22:37-40 KJV

This is no different from racism...faulting a person for being different and imposing your twisted beliefs on others. Who gave you the power to determine who a person should love in their private quarters? Do you understand that when you impose these things on your neighbor, you are imposing them on God as our love is God within us? In the verse above, Jesus blatantly says that these two things are inseparable. When a person goes into their private homes, your bigoted biases have no place in their space. When those doors close, what happens in their boudoir is no business of ours, just like with what happens in yours. Also, you cannot pick and choose what you believe in in this particular regard. All people are deserving of love. You, in effect, are denying a person their right to love, God's Love, and the aforementioned happiness God's Love brings. You are denying God love, God's Love and to love God's Love in another. It's not about what you believe in; it's about what's right. You could fervently believe the sun is purple, but it doesn't make it right just because it's your belief, and you shouldn't impose that belief on others by enforcing laws based on this ridiculous belief. Simultaneously, the golden rule applies here...when you deny a person anything that is their God-given gift, you are depriving them of the godly love attached to it; thus, harming them and yourself spiritually. It's okay for you to be devout, but if any human isn't as devout as you or in the same way as you, they're now deemed "less than"? No, that is not true nor okay, and you would not want it done to you. Support people's right to love just like they have to support your right to be a bigot. They may not like it, but they don't infringe on your right to be stupid. It's your right to live your life ignorantly; just don't impose that ignorance on others because it's your hangup, not anyone else's to suffer through.

That's why we're here when it comes to subraces. White supremacists think they're superior when God made us *all* equal. The Bible has less than two instances (if that many as those times were only describing Jesus) where they used color to describe or determine subrace or ethnicity because it did not matter then. Racism is a social creation to establish and maintain that superiority. Since these same people want to tout Christianity, they are actually doing everything opposite of what the Bible really says. How convenient. Don't be a shitty human being because you have unresolved soul-level issues. That is no one's issue but yours. Life should be simple. Instead, simple-minded people make life unnecessarily hard for others, and for no godly purpose.

"There is neither Jew nor Greek, there is neither slave nor free, there is no male and female, for you are all one in Christ Jesus."
~Galatians 3:28 KJV

I give my greatest to others, so I expect the same in return as part of my advocacy of Duality, Reciprocity, and the Golden Rule. I do not judge others for the path they chose, but I will help those that seek my help to reach the right path their Souls need to tread in order to evolve and reach its full potential—no matter who they are or once were. As for the people I speak about in this book that are negative and perform negative acts, I am not judging them because I cannot deflect heinous feelings that I do not possess, but I am making their positions clear to them. Some may not know what they do because some may think the bad things they do are right if they were brainwashed into thinking those things are right in some way. We all choose one of the many paths on our journey, sometimes changing paths along the way, even the outright bad people or the good people with horrible actions on this earth, but only one path leads us to our Soul's salvation, however long that journey may take. This journey always ends with the impact we have made on other people's lives, and how we live determines if we have to come back and do this shit all over again if we did not make any impact at all.

Humanity's issue is its ego. We are not discussing the ego we associate with conceit or pretentiousness (which are actually symptoms of the ego, not the foundation), but the ego that controls us and governs our free will. Contrary to common human belief, we do not actually know what is good for us. God is never wrong, and we cannot just bluntly tell Her otherwise by disagreeing with or shunning everything She makes, thinking we can make or do something better. Over the past several millennia, we have gotten away from being spiritual and connected to our higher selves. As such, we have turned into a greedy and unfeeling race of people. We no longer live by the Golden Rule, and we certainly do not value life, especially others' lives, as much as we are supposed to. As many people agree, humans are inherently good, but their environments, self-interests, and spiritual strength are among many contributing factors as to how we treat and view one another and ourselves. Albeit, history has shown us that greed has birthed many innovations and strengthened macro-economies; it also showed us internecine acts based on greed can destroy worlds—from an individual's world to entire nations. When we do not act in correlation with duality and reciprocity established by the Universe, there is no way an individual and their Soul can evolve, leaving a humanity full of selfish, lost souls wreaking even more havoc on the planet and each other. It is the people who have risen above this lower-level vibration who will be able to lead humankind to Nirvana. Anyone can say they are a man or woman of our Creator or a thought leader, but it is proven in their everyday actions and thoughts as all of our actions and thoughts are interconnected and interdependent on each and every one of us humans. It takes every one of us to do our own work to make a positive impact for everyone else.

Love

"*There is no fear in love; but perfect love casteth out fear: because fear hath torment. He that feareth is not made perfect in love.*"
~ 1 John 4:18 KJV

Love is fluid. Love is kind. Love is unconditional. Love is beautiful, and, most importantly, it's free. Love is God. We create conditions upon it just like we create conditions upon God. It doesn't come out of the box in any other form. Just pure. Why have we imposed our selfish egos upon love? Damn, we're so fucked up that we even try to change what God already made perfect, as if love wasn't good enough at its purest inception. Hippies, and I use the term positively, had the right idea. Hell, if you think about it, Jesus was a Hippie. It's about love, pure love, and the natural actions that come from it. Woodstock was the ultimate homage to love. However, people made fun of them (and still do) but would call themselves Christian. So, shall I assume if Jesus were alive today, they'd make fun of him, too? How can you be mad at or humiliate someone for encouraging peace and love but condone fighting and war as normal? It's no wonder that there was problem after problem for the Woodstock revival, and it ended up not happening. Bass ackwards, that is. People are just not fully evolved in the feminine aspects of love; people are only concerned with the masculine definitions of love as it pertains to

154

the ego and the world of Caesar. Anytime something is feared or misunderstood (one and the same in this case, actually), people try to make it fit into what they feel it should fit into instead of trying to understand it. That's like being a person that cannot understand another culture. Instead of *learning* about the culture, they make fun of it, try to change it, or try to kill everyone in it to make it go away. We actively go out of our ways to do shit like this. Seriously! Even as I write this, I realize humans do the dumbest or the most difficult ass shit sometimes. Like, doing everything possible to ourselves and everyone else to be unhappy. Love is already pure and perfect in and of itself. We cannot taint it with everything negative then call it pure. Love is to be freely given—beyond color, beyond subrace, beyond gender and sexuality. For you "Christians," that means you cannot be bigots (why am I having to keep saying this?). You cannot say you embody God's Love then don't wear a mask or discriminate against people that do not act or look like you. You are the living example of hypocrisy and absolutely what's wrong with Christianity. All the things that you purposefully do to stop people from living the lives God made for them because you disagree does not come from a place of love. You are telling the victims of your callousness they do not deserve God's Love and the God's Love inside of them is not worthy of anything. How do you think God feels about your actions; and, you placing God's Love in the trash with your bigotry, rather than letting another person have it? If Jesus was here, would he be able to say he agrees that you live a completely pious, love-filled life as you claim? If you have ever turned your nose up at someone because of anything other than their actions, then you, Forrest, are *not* Christian and living completely through love.

I love everyone, as we all should. I, especially, love helping people, even those full of hatred. Some were taught hatred, others learned it over time. In either case, they can be helped if they're open to it. I'll also help anyone I can to gain their strength back. It's innate and doesn't go anywhere. It just gets overshadowed by fear. Fear is the sole cancer on this planet that's 100% curable with no chemicals. Faith and strength are the cure for fear. I applaud anyone who takes their strength back from the fear thief. I just cannot sit back and watch humanity get weaker from this contagious disease. People are waking up, but even more people are becoming zombies (brainwashed, drugged out, uneducated in life, etc.).

It is up to us to do better. It is up to us to employ the golden rule in every aspect of our lives to help others do better. It is up to us to live our best lives. We cannot be mad at the next person who does not support our lives or make it easy and happy for us. If we choose to only see the negatives in our lives, then we choose to live negative lives. If we see our lives as bad, it is up to us to make the necessary changes to make it good—unless this is how you are choosing to live, then continue to do you. Love can help us do this. Some people, surprisingly, are just miserable and actively refuse to be happy and fully love themselves or another. Although this is on their journey, they do not have a right to do things that negatively impact the lives of others. That is where the line must be drawn. Even in misery, we must be altruistic and loving in our ways as our individual actions and efforts are always energy that affects others, no matter how carefully unintentional. Love is God and we must be true to the God in ourselves and in everyone else.

"Love is but the discovery of ourselves in others, and the delight in the recognition."
~Alexander Smith

Faith and Happiness

We cannot get weak at any point, ever. No matter what life throws at us, we absolutely cannot lose faith in ourselves or in God. We are human and do have moments of weakness, but we are not meant to and must not remain in these energies and thoughts. What purpose does it serve our lives or our Souls to remain at a heavier, lower vibration and to continue to suffer? Why is this justifiable and okay? Think about all the people before us who persevered, all the great heroes in history, and the everyday and unknown unsung heroes who made contributions to society in their own way through their own struggles. There are many examples of people making beautiful impacts on humanity while never losing faith.

I implore everyone who hasn't already to watch the show, *Alaskan Bush People*. There are plenty of shows that showcase the lives of people who have struggles. However, this show is about a family's faith, perseverance and tenacity through their unbreakable bonds founded in love. It is about a family who chose to live the hard and rough bush life away from the world, but at every turn, there was always something that went wrong. There were constant tests of their faith, but they never lost it, not once. They remained strong, and they remained irremovable together. They are also really good people. They were always helping others, and because others often helped them, they never lost faith in humanity no matter how badly humanity treated

159

them. In season one, episode three, the family was struggling to get settled into their new community and get their home built before winter. In spite of some challenges with some of the townspeople, a group of them came out to lend a welcoming, helping hand. This is what humanity is about. The Browns respect the earth and the animals that live upon it, and, through all of their obstacles, they always took a second to give God reverence and thanks. Every single episode presented a lesson that we all could learn from, and it is a beautiful show about beautiful, strong humans. If more of humanity was like the Brown family and the people they bartered with to help each other survive on God's land, the world would be a better, more resilient place. Some watchers were critical and put down the show saying it cannot be real or talked about the family members. I do not care if these things are real or not or what the family members do off-camera; I only care about the lessons that each episode and the family teaches. We do not have much of that anymore on television as it is just entertainment that no one learns anything moral from like every show I had growing up—from cartoons to adult sitcoms. Matt's struggle with alcohol and the family's support of him is a glaring example of everything I have said in this book regarding how people should support and help others and not judge, despite the family having a stern view of alcoholism. There are real-life struggles in each season, and that makes the show more real than anything. The Browns are examples of faith, strength, how people should treat one another, and paying their blessings forward. It is a must-watch show. In season seven, episode seven, Mother Ami, who had been diagnosed with lung cancer and watching the family being sad and worrying about the outcome, said it as best and as pure as anyone else could have said it: "Life's for living...you can't let adversities and trials take away your happiness because it can

160

distance you from God." If that is not insurmountable faith and strength, I do not know what is.

I have encountered many types of people in my various work, and I have found that people have these unreal perspectives of their lives and of themselves. I always encourage everyone to seek whatever help they feel they need to reach their best and highest. However, in these encounters, I have found that there is an unnecessarily intrinsic worry about the next person, not realizing that the next person may have the same struggles that another wishes they had instead of their own. People worry about their parents' judgments, not understanding that their mindsets come from antiquated or misinformed knowledge. Some may want to be skinny because they image issues and feel that is what society wants from them, but there are petite individuals who wish they could gain weight and struggle with image as well. There are many instances when people wish they had a different life while others wish they had that person's life, like the aforementioned celebrities and influencers. We do not always see their true lives on camera, even if they say they are giving us everything. We also do not think about why we are trying to live up to other people's expectations. For our own happiness, we must focus on the right positive things in and about our own lives and not things we cannot change or things that are only applicable to others. We have to find our happiest points and the pure happiness within, but not if it is based on what other people have, want, or want for us. It will only lead to disappointment and contributing to establishing or increasing our anxieties and depression when these things are not achieved.

As plausible as just accepting being unhappy because it seems easier than changing sounds to any individual who has

161

spent their lives avoiding ameliorating their life for fear of short-term discomfort or embarrassment, it is actually impossible to be 100% happy without any change, or growth through that change. Very few people are 100% unconditionally happy, no matter what most may think. There is no such thing as conditional happiness. You either are completely happy, or you are not. Period! There is no such thing as, "I am happy when…," "I am only happy if…," or, "I will be happy if/when…" As I have already incessantly preached, one of the biggest issues humans have today is separating ego from soul. There is a substantial difference between the two, and only one can lead us to our own eternal salvation. This begins with letting go of old judgment paradigms. We create our own struggles by instituting these barriers or obstacles based on judgments from others and attempting to fake enjoying living in the confines of these judgments. These judgments take away the beauty of life and living in the moment, the individuality of others, and seeing the fullness of our and their own potentiality. We must let go of these judgments, stigmas, and other negative confining boxes that serve us in no way. In keeping these things going, in effect, we become part of the problem in the world that keeps us stunted from growth, remaining the version of humankind that we are and to one another.

Sometimes, the path to happiness is a lonely one, but it is also an incredibly important internal one. It is wonderful to grab hold of our mental health instabilities as it pertains to our emotions and moods. It is even better to seek help in reaching the right mental health path to happiness, which comes in different forms for different people. However, some people get stuck in the position of acknowledging but never moving on to the next step of actually fixing. *Dealing* is only a temporary step. Some get mental health treatment to include medication management. Okay, awesome if it helps one deal *while* they try to fix. But, a lot of people never make it past dealing. Why "deal" with mental health imbalances for the rest of your life when these imbalances can be fixed and eliminated for good? Some people adamantly defend their mental health illness or give excuses when I ask them this question. Most of the people who defend tell me to go suck a railroad spike because I added more work for them to do that was already hard enough for them to start doing in the first place. They found a reason for the problem so they stick with that. For example, they may have found out they are bipolar after all these years of mood swings and they are satisfied with that and have changed their entire lives in order to suitably live with the diagnosis. Others want to continue to bury the things that caused the problems and faking or tricking themselves and others into believing they are okay as they have been doing all along. Unmasking trauma is an important step on the road to happiness. It cannot be attained by accepting the barrier that stands between you and happiness.

We fight tooth and nail for the things that are right in front of us or the wants that may not be in our best interests, but we give up on doing the positive work to attain the priceless yet grossly misunderstood things that are attainable and free, such as complete happiness, pure love, and unwavering faith, simply because they are not tangible. I cannot stand idly by while the people I love do this, no matter how harshly I know I will be treated for giving them the overall truth of these things. It is not that I am totally wrong when I say these things; it is because they are not ready to hear these things. We hold fast to what we know or believe (or want to fully believe) to be available and true but won't give ourselves the chance to have something godly that requires a bit of work and changing some of those beliefs. Remember the old adages say that not all things that are easy are good and things worth having are worth the effort. I can lead people to that shore, but most people are too scared to swim in the waters of faith, love, and happiness, then blame me or others if they drown on land. Okay. Well, have fun. I'll be over here breast stroking in my happiness. I don't claim to have all the answers for everyone, but I do know what it takes to get to eternal happiness because I fought so much and so hard to get here and remain here. Eternal happiness is very possible to achieve, as I have already said, but many people believe complete happiness to be an elusive, nonexistent unicorn. It is as real as anything tangible, like the inanimate things we have placed an expected happiness value on (alcohol, cars, celebrities' lives, drugs, money, murder, clinicians, other people; this list goes on). Also, because some people have inner demons they constantly fight, they do not want to look within to find that happiness, or they wholeheartedly believe it cannot and can never exist in there. We keep allowing ugly inner demons to flourish so happiness cannot exist within. Do you honestly believe that demons can lead you to happiness at some point? When has a demon *ever* made it its business to do that? So, what do we do? We let the ugly inner demons remain to never make room inside for complete happiness to blossom because we are too afraid to face those low energy things to get rid of them. It is up to each person in this struggle to make the decision to not let this happen. It is not up to any of those external people or things to replace or provide faux happiness or do the work for you.

People who are happy do not complain or blame others for anything, especially their unhappiness. Completely happy people understand that no one can affect or change what's within them unless it is allowed by the beholder. And, completely happy people do not do any of the above counterproductive actions because they guard that happiness and value it vehemently. Unhappy people do the exact opposite because unhappiness is the only condition familiar to these people, so it is easier to accept and to maintain, even though it is much harder to deal with. Think about what Bob Ross, Mister Rogers, and Mother Teresa would say about everything going on today. Would they agree with racism or how we view ourselves and treat others?

True happiness is attainable. It just depends on the amount of work one is willing to put in for this perfect gift and how much faith we have in ourselves and God to attain it. It has been found that people who are happier live healthier, longer lives. From a spiritual standpoint, we cannot live fully and fruitfully if we are consumed by heavy, maddening unhappiness and misery. There is no room for happiness when we are like this. If you have a cluttered attic, nothing else will fit, and too much weight could possibly result in a cave-in. Apply that to the human experience...when things are piled high, and we internalize all of this, the only way to relieve oneself of it is by choice (cleaning out the attic) or by the Universe's force (an implosion or explosion of bad actions and emotions). Throughout my life, I have experienced the Universe coming in to do the things I refused to do or could not see my way clearly to do. When the Universe had to step in, it was never pleasurable, but it was for my own good. I wish I had someone to lead me this way so I could have saved myself countless painful events. However, these were learning experiences that have led me here to be who I am today to help others. This goes back to my previous point: if we do not live the life we are supposed to, it only creates more insanity.

"Even if things don't unfold the way you expected, don't be disheartened or give up. One who continues to advance will win in the end."
~Daisaku Ikeda

Just *be* happy and stop giving excuses not to be, no matter the trials one endures. Everyone has the opportunity to be happy as happiness is free and cannot be taken by anyone unless we give it away or allow adversities and people to take it from us. Various parts of society have spent centuries creating ways of bulldozing straightforward avenues toward happiness boulevard or purposely setting up detours and roadblocks so that no one ever gets here, with many confused and lost travelers sitting together in misery on the roadside. Don't be lost without your roadmap back to happiness, no matter where you exit. We are our own cartographers. We are the weavers of our own webs. This is the end of this book...but it is the beginning for you!!!

"All things are mirrors in which you see yourself reflected, and the gloom which you perceive in your work is but a reflection of that mental state which you bring to it."
~ James Allen

About the Author

On July 28, 1980, I was born under the Leo Sun, for which I strongly identify with the traits of this zodiac. Growing up, I lived in a broken household. My mom was very abusive in my early life, and I didn't know my father until he showed up in my late teenage/early adult life. She told me that I looked like my dad and she despised him, so everything she hated about him, she took out on me. At seven or eight years old, I was called whores, sluts, maced, told that she wished I was dead, other wishes, and many fun names. The brawls, chokings, weapons, airbourne pots of boiling water or hot food, and fire-starting after I went to sleep manifested later and continued in my pre-teen and teenage years. All because of him. One of my favorite maternal aunts was the one who pretty much gave me the love I was missing but I, unfortunately, I still had to raise myself. She was the only one who showed me what unconditional love truly is. The rest of my family was estranged and only tolerated me at that time because I was a child or they were paid to. I was always being shipped off somewhere so my mother did not have to look at my gorgeous face. I did not have the chance to experience the lifelong joy of having a grandmother as she died the early morning of Thanksgiving when I was eight. Aunts and uncles that used to bounce me on their knees died around the same holiday time or just before Christmas in the following years. The trend of losing family members on or around holidays became my norm, so I stopped celebrating them early in life. I was rarely hugged or encouraged to be great, so I hated hugging as I got older. I did not know hugging was normal then but now I give fantastic hugs. I spent all of my time outside of school alone, reading about various things and writing poetry. Because I buried myself in books, my intelligence put me beyond where my peers were, so I was bullied and taunted for being a nerd. As I got older, I began to realize I was different from everyone else. I enjoyed school a lot because it was an escape, and I liked girls instead of boys. A double whammy. This only made my youth even harder. Coming up in Catholic school through senior year and a very religious environment, I had to deeply hide my feelings and ways of being who I truly was. I became depressed and suicidal at a very young age. I made many attempts, only to be disappointed in my failures to even do that right. So, I continued to throw myself into books and writing. By middle school, I had found a new love and lots of light in volunteering for causes geared to those less fortunate. The profound positive emotions I received from giving was a feeling I had never experienced before in my short life. It felt so good and so warm to my already cold and weary twelve year-old Soul.

By the time I reached high school, my problems had worsened but I met the most amazing group of people that made those years less dramatic than it could've been. I was in several car accidents. The worst one up until then was in my senior year with a classmate I was riding with to school that caused damage to my neck. Eventually, as I aged, the damage from the injury gradually affected the nerves that control my arms, causing problems with my hands and my ability to write. Just a few short weeks after that accident, I had contracted a virus that caused a double inner ear infection. The infection ended up taking away my hearing in both ears, and there was constant vertigo, so I could not walk on my own and I vomited every time I moved. This lasted for months. My "father" decided to show up and be one at this point, after Mom of the Year told me for many of my younger years that he died in his sleep just so I would never know how shitty he was as a dad. Bittersweet in hindsight, I guess. He took me to most of my doctor appointments during this annoying crisis. As time went on, we tried to build a relationship, but more on this later. I was very sick from the symptoms of this infection, missing one semester and a short part of the next semester of my senior year, when I thought for sure I would not graduate. After extensive testing for infections and diseases, like MS, it was found that I had developed Meniere's Disease, which is a rare disease that comes out of nowhere or from an infection, as in my case, and has no specific treatment for the hearing loss, extreme tinnitus, or vertigo that I still suffer greatly from to date. Although I was still very sick, I returned to school. I found out that I was now disliked and ostracized by my closest classmate friends for a rumor that was spread by the chick I was in the car accident with. I had no clue of these happenings during my lengthy absence, but I discovered quickly where I stood. In the face of all of this hell, I was able to power through and graduate on time, notwithstanding the permanent hearing loss in my left ear and continuing trouble with the other. However, the stellar grades I had worked so hard to maintain over the previous eleven years had suffered greatly. Prior to this, I had been accepted to the school of my choice in New York, but I was so discouraged that I regretfully chose not to attend. Also, this was a very formative time for me. With adults and people I'm supposed to trust letting me down at every turn so early on, I had finally witnessed for myself that there are beautiful, caring people still left in the world, and this gave me hope for the good left in humanity.

I worked laborious jobs while all of my friends and other peers matriculated, graduated, and became successful in their careers. I always loved the world of business and became obsessed with becoming an entrepreneur. So much so, that I quickly moved up into management positions at every job I held. Also, during this time, while my network of peers were following what society says is the right path to take (get a degree, marry, get a house with a white picket fence and dog, have 2.5 kids, retire, then die the next morning), I used my free time to travel and experience more of life and the world, as I was not able to do so growing up. Finally, things seemed to be serendipitous and going in the right direction for a short while, until I lost my aunt in 2004 after watching her slowly die for four months.

After a period of extreme depression and getting in very unhealthy relationships, I decided to start my own business as a financial consultant—later on in my story, growing it into a multifaceted, multi-location business that I have since scaled back to do more of my part for humanity. I took a leave of absence from my full-time job at that time for a couple of weeks to give it a try, and I was successful with it over that short period of time. This gave me hope, but I was too afraid to take the definitive leap of letting go of the security of my job. So, I only did it part-time for a few years. After this, the relationship I was in was over, so I went into deep depression again. I was not happy at all with my life. I knew I was supposed to be doing something great but I could not figure out what. As the next few years passed, working at jobs I hated and was unfulfilled in, I thought I was in a beautifully happy relationship until I found out I was the only one in it. I ended up marrying this person in October of 2010, only to spend my Thanksgiving and New Year's alone while they spent it with their "significant" other. The marriage was annulled in March of 2011. Over the years, my mother and I finally worked to ameliorate our tumultuous relationship. Shortly after my annulment, mom told me she had breast cancer. Since it was just us for the bulk of my life with me not having any other strong family connections, and for all of our interpersonal hardships, we began to mend our differences as her mortality became real. During this time, she admitted to me what I had long suspected—she had unresolved mental health issues from the traumas she sustained as a child herself. At the point in time, we were no different. We shared a common foundation. The sole difference is that I did not succumb to these circumstances and become the very person she was. However, this helped me see her differently, and it made forgiveness of her abusive treatment of me much easier. Simultaneously, I had finally been forced to seek professional help in fixing my anger issues and severe depression after I was sent to a psych ward for getting into a colorful, heated argument with my boss. I was diagnosed with depression, PTSD, and social anxiety. The medications only exacerbated those issues, and I hated every minute of the treatment and my life. My first experience with the efficacy of the mental health treatment available at that time and was not productive, promising, or therapeutic whatsoever. The now unlicensed psychiatrist, who told me I should be an addict—like the bulk of his clients, or a psycho- or sociopath with all the trauma I've endured, wasn't really that helpful…apparently, to anyone. Subsequent clinicians that attempted to help me were just as incompetent, uncaring, and unfeeling. Another practitioner in one of our best hospitals made it explicitly clear that her job was lucratively quantitative—she remains gainfully employed by the number of prescriptions she writes for big pharma and patients she can enroll in certain programs for the insurance payouts, government funding, and research; not her specific number of patients that live better, healthier lives simply because of integrated cognitive behavioral techniques or those

171

who fully recover from traumatic stress and other mental health ailments. Nothing seemed to help, except alcohol, which was introduced to me at a single-digit malt age. I decided to seek answers that weren't at the bottom of a bottle, and I was led further into the world of spirituality. I had already been interested in this world throughout the years but there was a very adamant internal push to hone my spiritual knowledge at this point.

For decades, I was taught to pray to Jesus and that he was the official incarnation of God. After further studying other belief systems—such as Buddhism, Judaism and the Kabbalah, and some Taoism, I realized there was so much more I did not know and what I believed in was all the way wrong. I remain an avid learner to date and student of all things Spiritual and Universal. This path helped me fan my flames. I eventually went on to finish school obtaining a few business-related degrees to figure out where I can best help humanity. I focused on international affairs, policies and human security so that I could help people in the world—not just at home in the States. I have worked on the advisory committees and boards of various global for-profits and nonprofits, and volunteered extensively with socioeconomically disadvantaged individuals—with many of the latter suffering from unaddressed psychological distress because of their situations. In wanting to do more than help these people gain and maintain economic and social sustainability, I wanted to help them to be able to overcome their mental anguish and birth new ways to maintain a healthy mindset so they do not fall back into the previous traps of despondency, vice abuse, or ongoing recidivism. I obtained further training and certification in professional counseling and psychotherapy. My areas of focus are addiction, mental health, grief, relationship counseling, LGBT+-related struggles, and sexual abuse. Additionally, I

172

provide coaching and counseling to entrepreneurs in business and finance. All of the education, training, and real-life experiences I have achieved and conquered allowed me to be the best and most effective entrepreneurial life and spiritual coach I can be in order to be the most impactful to others. I was able to start living my life differently with different perspectives without sacrificing who I truly am as I did for many years prior, all while still greatly helping those in the most need. There is no greater teacher than experience, so there is not much I have not gone through where I cannot be of some assistance to anyone at any time. We can always use a fresh perspective when we are clouded by what we're going through in order to get out of it. It is also good to know we are not alone during our tribulations. Throughout all of these decades and my own hardships, I never stopped giving of myself or volunteering for causes because it is a feeling like no other—God's pure love and true happiness and peace meshed with our own. Helping people reach their best gives me one hell of a high.

In the summer of 2019, I felt some familial changes reaching its apex. With these new perspectives I had cultivated over the last decade-plus and the level of growth I had reached by this time, I realized my relationship with my "father" was not what it used to be or what I needed from him if he were to continue in this role. After several arguments, which started in my hospital room after having complications from a major surgery in December of 2018, in trying to get him to understand that he could not treat me like I am a business transaction—like he was used to treating most people—I firmly told him that he was not being the father that I needed him to be to me. The irony is that he said that one of his other daughters from another relationship had this same complaint. Well, two completely

173

separate people cannot be wrong about the same exact thing. I gave him the chance to choose to be the father that he said he wanted to try to be or continue putting the rest of the world before me and one of his other daughters as he always had. Without hesitation, he chose the world; albeit, he will tell the world it was I who divorced him.

In April of 2020, my mother found out she had COVID19. When she was admitted, she was so ill that I could not speak to her on the phone, so her last words to me in a text message were, "I am so tired. I will be glad when I am well." She was intubated on April 13th, and after weeks of going up and down in improvement, she died on May 7th, 2020, after contracting pneumonia while sedated on a ventilator. That was probably the hardest three weeks of my entire life—having to get phone calls all day, every day, not knowing if that call was *the* call. I could not see or talk to her at any point during this time until they knew it was no more they could do. I was finally able to say goodbye to her the morning of May 7th. As I did, I watched tears roll down her cheek (she was still sedated). And, at that point, I knew she knew that was the last time we would see each other in the flesh. She was a Registered Nurse for 40+ years and had contracted the virus by helping seniors in her community learn more about the virus and ways of protecting and taking care of themselves when they otherwise couldn't where society had abandoned and failed them in these areas even before the pandemic. She had been sacrificing the PPE I and others had supplied her so others could be safe. Out of all of the heartache I had experienced in the whole of my life, including things not mentioned here, this was the most painful thing I have ever had to endure. I spent twenty three days not knowing if I was going to see my mother ever again when on the night of the twenty fourth day, she came to me in a dream to tell me how proud she was of me. She never looked happier as she was dressed in pure light. I could only find solace during this nightmare in the beautiful fact that she died doing what she was put here to do—taking care of others. This is the reason I am here now with this book. In full dedication to her calling and her passing, I will live the rest of my life doing the same, as I have been.

After over a year of non-communication with my mom's sperm donor, I decided to reach out to him to let him know she had passed. He did not answer, nor did he respond to my messages. I was very bothered by this. It took my wife to call him three weeks later, unbeknownst to me, to ask him if he ever got my messages for him to say that I abandoned him and severed our ties. With this position, he refused to put those things aside to maturely help me through my grief as any "father" would, notwithstanding any inane disagreements. He also called me more horrible things than anyone ever had in a very long time. This from the man who was never a father in action (at least not without me having to beg him to act like one), but only by namesake. No genuinely loving and unselfish parent would ever walk away when their child is suffering, no matter how old the child grows or what relationship difficulties arise. You never stop being a parent, especially if you were ever one to that person. Even though mom and I used to fight like ninjas in the street for years (weapons and all), she was always my mother. I could rely on her being by my hospital bed of her own volition. However, he only showed up because mom would guilt him into giving a fuck about these times (hence, why he showed up in my teens). He wasn't a parent in my life, especially when I needed him the most—like during this time of bereavement. So, I gave our relationship my final IDGAF shrug and lip purse, and this will be the last I would like to speak of that bitch. I tried.

For many years, I have been told that I needed to "tone" down or be nicer in my verbal interactions and representations; that I needed to regard how sensitive others might be. I remember being different as far back as preschool. One of my best and oldest friends from that era, whom I talk with almost every single day without fail, told me I have always been different and that is why we are still friends to this day (I love you, Mi!). Never have I ever been *intentionally* rude to people, but I certainly do not sugarcoat anything. This has been my personality since I could talk and walk at six months. Additionally, my playfulness is like garlic to some vampires. I am a very carefree person so I treat everything light-heartedly. Life is already absurdly difficult but I'm not going to be dry and stone-faced about it. I love to have fun, be happy, playful and smile. I allow the inner child that had to be an adult first to be free. Don't be afraid to pull your twisted knickers out 'ya crack and do the same. Life is too short for stoicism.

So, as I aged, I asked what about me...if this is my fire, why do I need to dim my flame and light just because others are too weak in theirs? I never had a problem with myself; it was always others who had a problem with me. I am who I am and I always went after what I wanted when society always told me I shouldn't or that I would never succeed in the endeavor. I was always told that I should conform and be quiet, and, in so doing, I ended up damaging myself and becoming just as weak as the people who were too sensitive or brainwashed to hear their own truths. That stopped when I realized it was making me physically ill to quiet my inner Lion. The naysayers should try going to the Serengeti and silencing the roar of a Lion short of killing it, and let me know how that works out for them. It is just not for me to be soft and sensitive after all of the full-on hell I endured for stretches of time. So I refuse to entertain that anymore in anyone, anywhere. Now, understand that I am not going around hurting people's feelings on purpose or disregarding any happiness they may feel before being disillusioned, but I am giving them the truth when they ask, despite how much it may hurt their feelings. Someone else being sensitive or not evolved enough to understand or want the message that they sought, is no longer my problem.

It is very rarely about how a message is conveyed but more about the strength of the recipient the message is for. If I were to tone myself down, then I would not be my authentic self living authentically; thereby, not being who I was truly born to be in executing God's Will for my Soul's Journey. There were numerous traumatic events that happened in the time between all those mentioned that also shaped my never-a-dull-moment life. I can't possibly enumerate all the times my life was in peril being on the streets of Baltimore City at a very young age, hiding in abandoned or condemned homes or under porches for shelter or if I was being chased; watching someone else's life-changing traumatic situation unfurl in front of me that I had to help them through; car accidents (I was a passenger all but once) over the years just narrowly missing being impaled or in a ditch at night in the middle of nowhere with no street lights and no shortage of undiscovered creatures, bleeding internally and unconscious for Lord knows how long; of being with someone I genuinely cared for, leaving, then, thirty minutes later, receiving a call the person was killed where we just shared our best laughs; burying friends my age as a teenager or young adult; or, watching someone take their last breath in my arms and witnessing their soul leave their body. However, through all of these tortuous events and many others, I realized I was put here to survive all this fun shit and be a candid voice of reason to those who seek it and those who need it, and to help people with my experiences. There is a substantial difference between willfully withholding good information in an attempt to spare the other person a tear or two and just being honest for that person's ultimate good. I always choose the latter. The former ends up creating more grief and hurting the querent more on their journey.

"You measure the size of the accomplishment by the obstacles you had to overcome to reach your goals."
~Booker T. Washington

Shout-Outs

Melona V- Thanks for driving me insane! I guess I couldn't have asked for a better partner to send me to the looney bin. I love you!

Paprika and Short Stuff- Being there for me during my time of grief meant the absolute world to me. Just that simple show of genuine love, in spite oe everything you both have going on in everyday life, and you taking the time out to do it anyway with no excuses or hesitation—it is what helped get me through; and, it's what I needed to remain strong. You guys have always been there for me and that's what makes you two the greatest in every way. Thanks for _always_ being there and being true! I love you guys, _always_!

Mimi- You already got your shout-out so pass this one along to Jhane, and hug my boys for me. I love you today, but I don't know about tomorrow. You stress me out.

Camille- I wish things would have been different on our journey but always know Scootie loves you beyond space and time.

Baker, The Lunch Table, Cheryl T, Kiersten, Michelle S, Sylvia, Shannon, Seifert, Jessica B, Shawna, Amy, Javan, Koretta, Andrea, Nelly Rock, Lakea, Terrica, Nicki M, Lucky, Lady M, Maria, Chrissy, Akia, Q, Lia, Tisa, Karla, all my Jens, Kellys & Melissas, Hogie, Nessa, Angie, Courtney, the love of my life- Blondie (Christy), all the angels we gained, and anyone else I missed- You're the most spectacular group of amazing ladies I could have had the greatest pleasure of spending my crazy and slutty SK years with, and you guys still being here tugs on my lil' ole' heartstrings. Large Marge Kenney, I wish you were here to read this, tell me how much I rambled then fuss me out because I rambled, right before you offer me a Marlboro to smoke with you in the music wing. You were one of my favorites, and I miss you. I love you all like blood to no end!

Adenike- You also drive me bananas. I guess it's also love...but, damn.

Mom- I miss the hell out of you, every damn second of every friggin' day! I hope I'm still making you proud. See you soon, my love...

Ruthie- Ignore your sister. She pushed my buttons, too. I sooooo miss you! I'll never stop.

Aunt Mae, Uncle John, Uncle Joe & Aunt Esther, Joanne, Sharon, Eva, Doc, Barry, & sometimes Tony, Sr.- Thanks for being there for me throughout my life. Love knows no distance or time.

Christ-In-A-Scripture, Daneen T., Miss Monk, Farrah, Tria, Rodney, Talawn, Yohn, Brandi P., Jody, Jezebel, Lady Lacey, Syreeta, James King, Kelli R., Mai Tai, Lo, Aunties Laura, Jeanette, Siney and Patricia, Dom, Mae, Chi, Linda P., the Madison Sisters, the Jacksons, and all of my other extended family and longtime personal friends- You all know I will always love y'all in my own special way.

Keiko & Pawsha, My Furbabies- Keiko, you're the best dog I've ever had. I am super blessed to have such an awesome, beautiful, intelligent, bad-ass over-protective bully sidekick that never leaves me, especially after destroying something expensive and hiding it under the couch thinking I won't find it. How can I *not* spoil you with all the love in the world? Pawsha, you're such a "B" with a capital "ITCH," but your absolute laziness and total I-don't-give-a-shit-you're-nothing royal cat-titude reminds me of my own innate leonine royalty. You both brought me back to life and taught me so much about living humanly. I love my little furry critters so much! Spoiled asses.

Everyone Else- Thanks for stopping by!

Live like royalty as humbly as a peasant, and just
_be_!

Books and Other Media I Enjoyed

1. The Celestine Prophecy ~ James Redfield

2. The Manual of the Warrior of Light ~ Paulo Coelho

3. Attaining the Worlds Beyond ~ Rav Michael Laitman

4. The Complete Works of James Allen

5. The Alchemist ~ Paulo Coelho

6. Empire State of Mind ~ Zack O'Malley Greenburg

7. Everything Written by Madam Helena Petrovna Blavatsky

8. The Book of Enoch

9. The Book of Thoth or Hermes Trismegistus

10. Sefer Yetzirah ~ Aryeh Kaplan

11. Sefer Zohar ~ Rav Michael Laitman

12. The Book of Raziel

13. The Key of Solomon

14. The Secret History of the World ~ Mark Booth

15. https://www.theatlantic.com/magazine/archive/1966/09/l
    sd-and-the-third-eye/361531/

16. Archie's Place S4E3: The Eyewitnesses—Raul and Jose
    sacrifice themselves with the risk of being deported back
    to a poor and violent country for the safety of those who
    do not look like them.

17. The Handmaid's Tale

18. Supernatural

19. The Original Suffragettes Were Not All White:
    https://www.history.com/news/black-suffragists-
    19thamendment

20. PBS Special Episode—Without a Whisper: Konnon:Kwe

References

1. https://www.newsweek.com/luxury-brands-prefer-burn-millions-dollarsworth-clothes-over-letting-wrong-1032088

2. https://www.washingtonpost.com/news/arts-andentertainment/wp/2018/01/19/hm-faced-backlash-over-its-monkeysweatshirt-ad-it-isnt-the-companys-only-controversy/

3. https://www.mit.edu/~rei/spirjesusname.html#:~:text=Most%20dictionaries%20will%20translate%20Jesus,a%20passive%20quality%20to%20God.&text=Yah%20is%20short%20for%20Yahweh,%2C%20save%20alive%2C%20rescue.%22